Karla ~

Health & Happiness,

Yoga: The Art of Balance

✦

A Practical Guide to Yoga for the 21st Century

Jim Gaudette

iUniverse, Inc.
New York   Bloomington

Yoga: The Art of Balance
A Practical Guide to Yoga for the 21st Century

iUniverse books may be ordered through booksellers or by contacting:

iUniverse
1663 Liberty Drive
Bloomington, IN 47403
www.iuniverse.com
1-800-Authors (1-800-288-4677)

ISBN: 978-1-4401-0168-7 (pbk)
ISBN: 978-1-4401-0169-4 (ebk)

Library of Congress Control Number: 2008939009

Printed in the United States of America

iUniverse rev. 11/24/2008

Table of Contents

To Deb

I would like to thank Priyanka Gaudette for her photography and Julie Webb, Christina Webb, Shane Stacy, Kristin Carlson, Caryn Shaw, Priyanka Gaudette, Jennifer Gaudette, Nancy McDermont, Michael Guckeen and Amara Jenkins for their modeling of the poses. Special thanks to Mia Murphy and Julie South for their review of the manuscript and suggestions.

Introduction

The purpose of Yoga is awareness, not perfected poses, beliefs, or any kind of attainment. Awareness from moment to moment requires quiet strength, flexibility, and balance. A good Yoga practice develops exactly these characteristics.

Before you start

When to practice depends on what your lifestyle permits. A morning practice is nice as there are fewer interruptions and it is a great way to start your day. An evening practice will refresh you from your day's activities and relieve the stress of the day. You can also do half in the morning and half in the evening. Afternoons are also fine except that most people don't have that time available. See what you enjoy the most and what you can continue on a regular basis. Regularity is the most important thing. A mixture of classes and home practice is very important for people just starting out.

It is best to practice on an empty stomach. Wait one to three hours after a meal depending on what and how much you have eaten. Listen to your body. It will tell you.

Drink water during your practice only if your body tells you that you need it. Drink as much water as you like after you finish.

Find a clean, flat area where you can practice undisturbed. Do not practice in a space that is too cold (under 70° F) as your muscles will be tight and prone to injury. If you cannot find a warm place, wear sweats or other warm clothing.

You will need a Yoga mat (sticky mat). These are available at any sporting goods store or department store. They are also available through the internet. The two most common props are blocks and straps. A block of wood and an old neck tie will also work.

Wear comfortable clothing that will stretch with you but not get in the way, giving you as much freedom of movement as possible. There are many Yoga fashions available in all price ranges in stores and on the internet. Special Yoga clothing is not necessary, although many practitioners prefer it. Men often wear gym shorts and a tee shirt. Make sure to practice barefoot as it is important to feel the mat or floor for traction and for feedback about your alignment.

If you have any medical conditions or are pregnant, please check with your doctor before beginning this or any other exercise program. Do not practice Yoga under the influence of alcohol or drugs.

General Rules for All Poses

1. Breathing

Breathe! Always breathe through the nose with a closed mouth. Do not hold your breath. Your breath should be like the ocean ebbing and flowing on a sandy beach. In vigorous poses, your breath should be like the high tide, with powerful waves slowly advancing up the shore, and then slowly and powerfully receding back. In restorative poses, your breath should be like the low tide, with gentle waves caressing the shore and then gently receding back again.

Although your conscious mind cannot directly control your emotions or autonomic body, it can control your breath. Your breath is the bridge between your mind, emotions, and autonomic body. Try being angry while you are breathing deeply. Breathe fast and shallow, and watch your heart rate increase. When you feel stressed or threatened, your sympathetic nervous system increases adrenaline production and heart rate, your digestive, reproductive and immune systems turn off, you breathe shallow and fast, your eyesight becomes more acute, your muscles tense, and you prepare for fight or flight. When you start deep breathing, your parasympathetic nervous system will calm your body and return it to a relaxed state so that it can function normally again.

It is important to breathe deeply and rhythmically during Yoga. When you inhale, you should feel your lower ribs expanding in the front, sides, and back. You should be aware of your intercostal muscles between your ribs stretching as you inhale. You should feel your lower ribs contracting as you exhale. Many instructors encourage the "three part breath", which is first filling your upper chest, then expanding your ribs, and then expanding your abdomen, and reversing on the exhale. (Some teachers teach this sequence in reverse order). Although this type of breathing is a good way to make you more aware of your breathing and what is going on while you breathe, it is not a good way to breathe during your Yoga poses because thoracic (upper chest) breathing tightens and restricts your upper body, shoulders and neck, and abdominal breathing encourages your lower back to sway forward. In most poses, your abdomen should be lifted in and up, not distended. Diaphragmatic breathing works best, as your breathing should always encourage relaxation and support good posture. (see Glossary)

You should try to inhale during opening motions and exhale during folding motions. For example, you inhale while raising your arms and exhale while lowering them and exhale while forward bending and inhale while straightening. (Inhaling while straightening protects your lower back). During twists, you extend the spine with your inhale and twist with your exhale. In most poses, extend and elongate with each inhale; release deeper and soften with each exhale. Make sure to continue slow, deep diaphragmatic breathing while you are in the poses.

Many people practice Ujjayi breathing during their Yoga practice. Ujjayi is Sanskrit for "victorious". The easiest way to learn this style of breathing is to say "HAAA" with an open mouth while exhaling and "AAAH" while inhaling. You will sound like Darth Vader. Now try this same technique with your mouth closed, breathing through your nose, making the same sound. This type of breathing elongates the breath and gives you better control of the air flow because of the increased resistance from narrowing the air path. It also naturally draws your attention to your breath because of the audible sound of your breathing. This helps you breathe smoother and is valuable feedback about your mind and body. Some people get it right away and some people need to practice a while. I encourage everyone to master this type of breathing and then decide for themselves whether or not they want to use it during their Yoga practice.

I cannot overemphasize the importance of breathing! You can go for weeks without food, days without water, but only a couple minutes without breathing. Without a constant supply of oxygen and a constant release of carbon dioxide, our cells die and the process that we call life ceases. The Sanskrit word for soul is "Atman". The German word for breath is "Atmen" They are both Indo-European languages with common roots. The Sanskrit word "prana" means both life force and breath. In the Old Testament, God gave Adam the "breath of life". Whether you consider breath sacred or a biological necessity, breathing is the single most important act in life.

2. Getting In and Out

When you begin a pose, focus first on your feet or that part of your body that is touching the floor. Make sure that the foundation of the pose is right. After you have established the foundation, move into the pose slowly and gracefully, watching your alignment as you go. Make sure that you start your alignment with your core, then shoulders and hips, elbows and knees, and lastly your hands and/or feet. From your core, work your way to the top of the head, the heels or toes, and the finger tips. Keep the back of your neck and spine long in most poses, remembering that your neck is part of your spine. Your entire spine, including your neck, should make a concave, convex, or straight line from the tip of your tailbone to the top of your head. Don't lock your knees or elbows.

Be aware of your "edges". Your minimum edge is where you first start to feel the muscles stretching and the maximum edge is where the sensation is intense but not painful. Once you are near your edge, open and extend from your core to your extremities. Feel the energy. Then, while still holding the energy, gently extend with every inhale and relax and soften with every exhale. Let go of any tension in your neck, your eyes, your jaw, or any other spot where you are holding tension or wasting energy. Learn to tell the difference between tension and energy. While in the pose, turn your attention inwards and ask: How do I feel? Where is my body tight and where is it relaxed? Where am I strong? Where am I flexible? Where am I vulnerable? Does this pose elicit any emotions? Learn about yourself. This is the real Yoga. The poses are only vehicles to get you there.

Start with three to five breaths and work up to ten. Once you can hold a pose for ten breaths, you can decide how many you want to do for each practice. Make sure to do the same number of breaths for each side of your body. More isn't necessarily better. Remember that you do not want to over or under stretch. Be aware and listen to your body.

When you are ready to come out of your pose, don't collapse or fly out of the pose. Come out slowly and with awareness, just like you went into the pose. Leave the pose as if you regret leaving a good friend, not as if you are trying to get away from something. Your breath is just as important exiting the pose as it was going into it.

If you feel pain during a pose, back off and breathe. If pain persists, tell a competent teacher and seek medical advice. You may be doing the pose incorrectly, have medical problems, or both. Remember: If you feel pain, you are hurting yourself.

For women only:

Some teachers believe that Yoga practice in general and especially inverted poses should be avoided during menstruation. There is no medical evidence to support this claim. Some women experience discomfort when doing poses during menstruation and some find that it offers relief from symptoms. Find out for yourself. Listen to what your body says right now, not what men said in ancient times.

Especially for men:

Although Yoga was practiced primarily by men for thousands of years, the majority of practitioners in the West are women. Men gain just as much from Yoga, and it is becoming more and more popular with athletes. Many professional sports teams now use Yoga as part of their training.

"Yoga has made my entire body more flexible. I'm stronger in my upper body, and I'm living proof that Yoga prevents injuries." – Eddie George, Heisman Trophy winner, NFL running back

"I've been doing Yoga since 1995, and I practice my breathing and focusing exercises before every game." – Kevin Garnett, NBA All-star

"In sports, you need balance, strength and flexibility, and Yoga helps so much in each of these areas. It's definitely been a huge part of my success." – Sean Burke, NHL All-star

Initially, men often need to concentrate more on flexibility and women on strength, but they both need the balance and stress reduction that comes right from the start. Whether you are a "burly man" or a "girly man", you get the same benefits. Yoga is especially important for men who do strength training (weight lifting) as it helps to lengthen the muscles that strength training shortens. This leads to additional strength, endurance, flexibility, and range of motion.

For everyone:

At the end of each practice, make sure to spend five to fifteen minutes in relaxation to eliminate fatigue and to absorb the benefits of the poses. A good relaxation will also help you come out of your practice feeling calm and full of energy.

Yoga is beneficial for both sexes, all races, ages, body types, creeds, and nationalities. Animals instinctively know the importance of stretching and stretch throughout the day.

Most importantly, have fun!!

The poses

I have broken the poses down into three levels. If you are new to Yoga or don't feel ready, do not do Level II or Level III poses. Go slowly and master the basic poses first. Once you feel confident in the basic poses, do both the basic level and Level II. When you feel ready to go on, do the basic level, Level II, and Level III. The "lower" levels are necessary warm ups for the "higher" levels and should not be omitted. If you want a shorter workout, omit an entire sequence or the higher levels, not the beginning part of a sequence. The only exception to this is the **Balancing** poses. You can do as many or as few as you want in any particular practice. Do not omit the initial **Mountain sequence** and **Sun salutations** or final **Relaxing sequence** as they are an integral part of almost any practice. The **Transition/re-aligning** poses are important bridges between the sequences. If at any time a sequence becomes too intense, you can do **Child** pose until you are ready to continue or omit the **Low plank** and **Up dog,** and go directly to **Down dog** from **High plank**. Follow the directions but pay attention to what your body is telling you. Unless you are specifically working on a particular pose, try to flow from pose to pose like a dancer. Think of each session as if it were all one slow motion dance or slow motion martial arts form (Karate kata, Tae Kwon Do poomse, or Tai Chi sequence).

Although you need to work on technique to master the poses, the technique is not the Yoga, just like the steps are not the dance and the notes are not the music. Do the dance; play the music; be the Yoga.

The photos in this book show various people doing the poses. You may or may not look like any of them. Each person is unique and will look slightly different in every pose. Find each pose in your own body, using the photos as guidelines. Read the instructions, look at the photo, and then try the pose.

Mountain Sequence

This sequence is a great way to start as it improves your posture, is good for asthma, opens your chest and shoulders, and gets your breathing going for the **Sun salutations**. The extended spine (your neck is part of your spine), tucked tailbone, and lifted abdomen create a feeling that you will replicate in many of the poses that follow.

Mountain *(Tadasana)*

Fig 1

- Stand at the front of your mat with your toes together and your heels slightly apart **Fig 1**. If you have lower back problems, standing with your feet hip width apart (with heels slightly wider than the front of your feet) can sometimes be beneficial as it opens your lower back.
- Lift your toes and spread them. Relax them.
- Lift your knee caps and thighs. Do not lock your knees.
- Tuck your tailbone and lift your abdomen in and up.
- Extend your spine from your tailbone to the top of your head.
- Lift your rib cage. Get tall.
- Roll your shoulders up and back, and then relax them. Make sure that your thumbs are facing forward.
- Extend your neck and slightly lower your jaw, extending the back of your neck a little more.

- Push up with the top of your head as you push down with your feet.
- Look straight ahead. Stay tall and relaxed.
- Start slow, rhythmic Ujjayi or deep breathing through your nose. Feel your lower ribs extending out with each inhale and contracting back with each exhale like bellows.

Extended Mountain A *(Urdhva Hastasana A)*

Fig 2   **Fig 3**

- On your next inhale, raise your arms up to shoulder height on each side, palms facing down **Fig 2**. Reach as far as you can in both directions. This is active and energetic, yet relaxed. Make sure that your shoulders remain relaxed.
- Exhale as you turn the palms of your hands upwards **Fig 3.**

Fig 4

- On your next inhale, raise your arms straight up over your head **Fig 4**. (By lifting your arms in this manner, you open your upper back). Straighten your elbows, but don't lock them. Your palms should be facing each other and your shoulders should be relaxed. Keep your tailbone tucked and your abdomen lifted in and up. Breathe.
- Exhale your arms back to your sides.

Extended Mountain B *(Urdhva Hastasana B)*

Fig 5

- Inhale your arms up half way **Fig 2**.
- Exhale your palms up **Fig 3**.
- Inhale your arms overhead with your palms touching **Fig 5**. You may cross your thumbs if you like. Relax your shoulders as you extend your spine and arms. Keep your abdomen lifted and tailbone tucked. Breathe.
- Exhale your arms back to your sides.

Extended Mountain C *(Urdhva Hastasana C)*

Fig 6

- Inhale your arms up half way again.
- Exhale your palms up.
- Inhale your arms overhead and interlace your fingers.
- Turn your palms up keeping your fingers interlaced **Fig 6**. Relax your shoulders as you extend your spine and arms.
- Push up with the palms of your hands as you push your feet into your mat. Keep your abdomen lifted. Breathe.
- Exhale your arms back to your sides.

Crescent moon *(Triyaktadasana)*

Fig 7

- Inhale your arms up.
- Interlace your fingers and turn your palms up.
- Slowly exhale to the right, forming a crescent shape **Fig 7**. Keep your hips squared, your neck long and your chin up. Lift your knees and straighten elbows. Push your left heel into the floor. Stretch long and reach. Do not collapse or let your left shoulder roll forward. Imagine your body between two walls or two planes of glass. It is not important how far to the right you go. It is important how much you stretch the left side of your body. Feel your intercostal muscles between your ribs stretching with each inhale. Keep breathing. Get longer with each inhale and soften with each exhale. Breathe.
- Inhale back up and repeat on the left side. Inhale back to **Extended Mountain C** and exhale your arms back to your sides.

Sun Salutation Sequence

Sun salutations Fig 8-19 are an excellent way to warm up as they build heat and stretch your entire body, preparing it for more strenuous poses and deeper stretching. The heat that this sequence builds will help prevent injuries and improve circulation. **Sun salutations** are not only a great start to a Yoga session; they are also a nice way to wake up your body/mind first thing in the morning. A complete **Sun Salutation** is pictured first with the individual poses and explanations following.

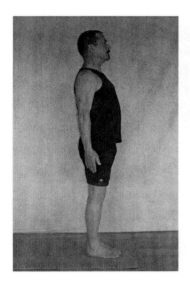

| **Fig 8** | **Fig 9** | **Fig 10** |

Fig 11

Fig 12

Fig 13

Fig 14

Fig 15

Fig 16

Fig 17

Fig 18

Fig 19

Gentle back bend

Fig 20

- From **Extended Mountain A** inhale and gently bend backwards **Fig 20**. Stretch long. Look at the ceiling. As you are just starting to warm up, only bend gently back, with more emphasis on lifting your rib cage and stretching your front than bending your back.

Forward bend *(Uttanasana I)*

Fig 21

- Exhale through a swan dive (arms extended to both sides) to **Forward bend**, folding from the hips, not the waist **Fig 21**. If you have very tight hamstrings or lower back problems, soften or slightly bend your knees. Keep your abdomen lifted and your spine long as you fold forward.
- Once folded, relax your neck and look at your knees. Touch the floor with your finger tips if you can. Eventually you will probably be able to press your palms to the floor. Do not force. You should feel your hamstrings gently stretching. You should not feel any discomfort in your lower back. If you do, back off and bend your knees.

Forward arch *(Uttanasana II)*

Fig 22

- Inhale your head and shoulders up to parallel with the floor with a long straight back and place your hands on your knees or shins **Fig 22**. Keep your neck long as you look at the floor. Feel your back extend and your hamstrings stretch.
- Roll your shoulders back and down as you extend your spine.
- Rotate your pelvis so that your tailbone and your lower back are on the same plane, making one long line from the tip of your tailbone to the top of your head.
- Broaden your shoulders making space between your ears and your shoulders.

Lunge

Fig 23

- Exhale your right foot back to **Lunge Fig 23**. Keep your left foot flat on the floor with your left knee directly over your ankle. Your finger tips should be on the floor. If it is too difficult to hold this position, you can lower your right knee to the floor.
- Lower your hips and straighten your right leg.
- Roll your shoulders back, lift your chest, and look forward. Try to make a long straight line from your forehead to your right heel.

High plank *(Adho Mukha Dandasana)*

Fig 24

- Inhale your left foot back next to and hip width from your right foot **Fig 24**. If this is too difficult, lower your knees to the floor. Your hands should be flat on the floor with spread fingers (middle finger facing forward) beneath your shoulders. Make a long straight line from the top of your head to your heels (or from the top of your head to the end of your tailbone if you lowered your knees).
- Looking at the floor, lengthen your arms without locking your elbows, make space between your shoulders and your ears, and broaden your chest and shoulders keeping your abdomen lifted in and up. Make sure that your seat is neither sagging nor too high. You need to be one long straight line. If you have wrist problems causing pain in this pose, **Low plank**, **Up** and **Down dog**, use a wedge under the palms of your hands **Fig 25** or hold the handles of dumbbell weights **Fig 26**.

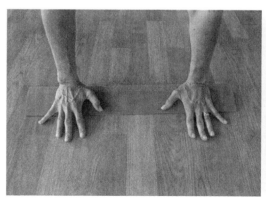

Fig 25

Fig 26

Low plank *(Chaturanga Dandasana)*

Fig 27

- Exhale, lowering your body to pushup position **Fig 27**. Keep your elbows right next to your ribs. Your entire body should remain in the exactly the same position as **High plank** (including knees on floor if needed) except that you have bent your elbows to lower yourself. If you can hold this position without touching your body to the mat, do so.

Up dog *(Urdhva Mukha Svanasana)*

Fig 28

- Inhale your upper body up as you go from your toes to the top of your feet **Fig 28**. Reach long with your arms, roll your shoulders back, lift your chest, and look forward. If you can lift your legs off the floor, do so.
- If this position is too difficult, do **Cobra (Fig 86)** instead of **Up dog**.

Down dog *(Adho Mukha Svanasana)*

Fig 29

- Exhale your feet back to the balls of your feet on the floor and your seat up and back for **Down dog Fig 29**.
- Straighten your legs without locking your knees. If straightening your legs is too difficult or painful, bent knees are fine. Try to get your weight centered more on your legs than your arms.
- Lift your sitting bones, extend your arms, and broaden your chest, lifting your abdomen in and up towards your spine. Your hands should be three to four feet from your feet, depending on the relative length of your torso, arms, and legs.
- Relax your neck while looking between your feet. Try to move your upper body down and back without moving your hands, making an upside down letter "V".
- Lower your heels. Getting your heels to the floor is neither the object of this pose nor even possible for everyone. It is more important to try to get your sitting bones up high and a long straight line from the top of your head to the bottom of your tailbone.

Lunge

Inhale your right foot forward for **Lunge**, repeating as before.

Forward bend *(Uttanasana)*

Exhale your left foot forward for **Forward bend**, repeating as before.

Chair or Fierce *(Utkatasana)*

Fig 30   **Fig 31**

- Inhale your seat down to a sitting position while you lift your arms with straight, not locked elbows and facing palms **Fig 30**.
- Look forward while lowering your hips and stretching your arms up. Keep both feet flat on the floor and your shoulders and neck relaxed. Breathe. You may want to stay for several breaths in this pose. (Optional: Open your mouth wide and stick your tongue as far out and down as you can **Fig 31**).

Mountain *(Tadasana)*

On an inhale, straighten back up to **Extended Mountain A**. Exhale your arms down to **Mountain**.

In second sun salutation:

Level II Lunge/Plank Sequence

These additions to the **Sun salutation sequence** will add deeper stretching and twisting as well as building additional core strength.

A - Elbows to floor *(Utthan Pristhasana)*

Fig 32

Fig 32A   **Fig 32B**

- After each **Lunge**, inhale as you lower your straight leg knee and the top of your foot to the floor.
- Exhale your hands flat on the floor to the inside of your forward foot and lower your upper body forward until both elbows (or hands if elbows don't reach) are on the floor **Fig 32**. Look at the floor. Breathe.

B - Arms up *(Anjaneyasana I)*

Fig 33

- Inhale your upper body up with arms reaching tall and palms facing **Fig 33**. Relax your shoulders as you extend your arms, palms facing.
- Lower your hips and lift your ears. Feel the energy going up your arms. Look forward. Breathe.

C - Back bend *(Anjaneyasana II)*

Fig 34

- Exhale your arms back for a gentle back bend, trying to keep your biceps next to your ears **Fig 34**. Remember, you are not totally warmed up yet. Go easy and don't overdo it. Lift your ribs as you extend your spine. Be aware of your lower back and avoid overextending it.
- Look at the ceiling. Breathe.

D – Twist *(Parivrtta Parsvakonasana)*

Fig 35

- Inhale back to upright and with a tall straight back make prayer hands with thumbs at the center of your chest.
- Exhale while twisting your opposite elbow to the outside of your bent knee **Fig 35**. As with all twists, start from your core, then your chest, shoulders, and finally your head. Keep your thumbs on your sternum. Look back, but go easy on your neck. (If you have neck problems, look to the side of the room). Breathe.
- Inhale back to center and exhale your foot back to **High plank**.

E – Side plank *(Vasisthasana)*

Fig 36

Fig 37

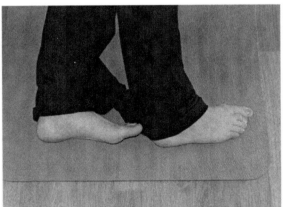

Fig 37A

Fig 38

- After **High plank**, lower your left knee to the floor.
- Inhale your right arm up and look at your right thumb **Fig 36**. (If you have neck problems, look straight ahead). Your left hand should be directly below your left shoulder and there should be a straight line from wrist to wrist.
- If this isn't challenging enough, try it with straight legs and your feet next to each other **Fig 37** or stacked on top of each other **Fig 38**.
- Extend both arms and extend your body from your heels to the top of your head. Breathe.
- Exhale your upper arm down to start **Side plank** on the other side or **Back plank Fig 39**. After your second **Side plank**, return to **High plank,** and finish the **Sun salutation.**

F – Back plank (Level III) *(Purvottanasana)*

Fig 39

- Keeping your left hand where it is, exhale as you rotate your body and lower your right arm to the right side of your body. Place your hands shoulder width apart with your fingers facing your feet, palms flat on the floor.
- Inhale your arms long and straight while lifting your hips **Fig 39**.
- Open your shoulders, open your chest, lift your hips, and try to put your feet flat on the floor. Keep your legs straight while extending from your toes to the top of your head. Look at the ceiling. Don't let your neck collapse back. Breathe.
- Turn your right hand fingers facing forward and inhale your left arm up for **Side plank** on the other side, return to **High plank,** and finish the **Sun salutation.**

In third sun salutation:

Triangle Sequence

The Triangle sequence is great for stretching and strengthening your thighs, knees, ankles, abdomen, buttocks, and spine. It opens your chest and shoulders, and improves balance and coordination. It also relieves stress and improves digestion.

Triangle – left side *(Trikonasana)*

Fig 40

Fig 40A

Fig 41

Fig 41A

- After **Down dog,** look forward and inhale your right foot 2/3 of the way to your hands. (The photos show the left side.) Make sure that both feet are flat on the floor and both your front foot and knee are facing directly forward. Your feet should be about 3 feet apart.
- Turn your back foot to 45 degrees. Make sure that both feet are lined up and flat on the floor before inhaling up to standing with straight legs. Lift your knees and thighs.
- Stretch your arms long, one forward and one back making one long line from the finger tips of one hand to the other. Your shoulders need to be relaxed and your back shoulder should not slump forward. Keep your tailbone somewhat tucked and your abdomen lifted so you don't have a sway back.
- On your next exhale, tilt your pelvis, lowering your front hip as you reach your forward arm as far forward as possible without strain **Fig 40**. Reach with your ribs as well as your arm. Don't let your back shoulder roll forward.
- Inhale as you lower your right hand to your knee, shin, or foot and lift your left arm.
- Turn your head and look up at your left thumb, keeping the back of your neck long **Fig 41**. (If you have neck problems, look to the side of the room). Keep your left shoulder back and the straight line from hand to hand. Open your chest. The lower side of your body should be as long and straight as the upper side with a long straight line from the tip of your tailbone to the top of your head. Feel the energy going up your arms, down your legs, and up your spine. Breathe.
- Inhale back to standing, keeping your arms and shoulders in a long straight line.
- Exhale as you windmill your arms down to **Lunge**. Continue with an inhale to **High plank,** exhale to **Low plank,** inhale to **Up dog,** and exhale to **Down dog** before looking forward and inhaling your left foot forward for the **Triangle Sequence** on the other side. Finish with **High plank, Low plank, Up dog, Down dog,** look forward and jump or walk your feet between your hands before grabbing your elbows in **Forward bend Fig 47**. Keep your neck relaxed and feel your hamstrings stretch without tension in your lower back. If you have lower back problems, slightly bend your knees. Breathe.
- Slowly inhale as you roll up one vertebra at a time to **Mountain**.

Fig 42

Level II Half moon – left side *(Ardha Chandrasana)*

Fig 43   **Fig 43A**

Fig 43B

- After each **Triangle**, instead of inhaling back to standing, exhale and lower your raised arm to the floor while bending your front knee.
- Using a block if needed **Fig 43**, place your right hand (left the second time, as in the photos) about one foot in front of your forward foot and slightly to the outside of your baby toe.
- Inhale as you straighten your front leg (without locking your knee), then lift and extend your back leg with lots of energy through the ball of your back foot. Go slowly.
- Exhale as you rotate your upper hip perpendicular, then roll your shoulder back and inhale as you lift your upper arm, making a straight line from hand to hand, and from the ball of your back foot to the top of your head. Open your chest.

- With the back of your neck long, look up at the thumb of your raised hand **Fig 43 A,B**. (If you have neck problems, look to the side of the room). Feel the energy in your legs, arms, and spine. Breathe. When you begin this pose, it is helpful to practice against a wall with both hips and both shoulders against the wall in the finished pose. After you have the feel of the pose against the wall, you can start with just straightening your front leg, and then add lifting your leg, stacking your hips etc one step at a time. Master one step and then go to the next. Go slowly.
- After each **Half moon** return to **Triangle** before continuing.

Level III Revolved half moon – right side *(Parivrtta Ardha Chandrasana)*

Fig 44

- After each **Half moon**, while still in the pose, exhale as you lower your raised arm until your hand is about one foot in front of your front foot and slightly to the outside of your front big toe, using a block if needed.
- Keeping your front leg straight and your back leg lifted and extended, inhale your right arm (left the second time) up, making a straight line from the ball of your back foot to the top of your head and another from hand to hand **Fig 44**. Open your chest.
- Look up at the thumb of the lifted hand keeping the back of your neck long. (Again, if you have neck issues, look to the side of the room). Breathe.
- Exhale your upper arm back down and inhale your other arm back up to **Half moon**, then **Triangle** before continuing.

Level III Revolved triangle – right side *(Parivrtta Trikonasana)*

Fig 45

- From **Triangle**, square your hips facing forward, angle your back foot closer to parallel with your front foot but still at an angle, exhale your upper arm down and place that hand on your knee, shin or foot. Make sure that both legs are straight and your spine is long and extended before twisting.
- Inhale your other arm up making a straight line from hand to hand, shoulders included **Fig 45**. Open your chest. Look at your thumb on your raised hand. (If you have neck problems, look to the side of the room). Breathe. In reverse order, go back to **Triangle** before continuing **Sun salutation**.

In fourth sun salutation:

Side Warrior Sequence

This sequence stretches and strengthens legs, ankles, groins (psoas), spine, shoulders, chest, and lungs. It increases stamina, relieves backaches, and stimulates abdominal organs. It is great for overall strength and endurance.

Side Warrior or Warrior II – left side *(Virabhadrasana II)*

Fig 46

- From **Down dog,** look forward and inhale your right foot between your hands.
- Exhale your back foot to a 90 degree angle keeping your back leg straight with the knee facing the side of the room and front knee directly over your front ankle with that knee facing straight forward and inhale your torso up to **Side Warrior Fig 46** with palms facing down, long arms, and relaxed shoulders. If it is too difficult to go into **Side Warrior** in this way, you can first inhale up to standing and then lower your torso into the pose. (The left side is pictured.)

- Make sure that you are not leaning forward and that your tailbone is tucked and abdomen lifted. Your spine should be straight from the top of your head to the tip of your tailbone without a sway back. Your front foot should be facing straight forward and the arch of your back foot should line up with the heel of your front foot. Your body should be facing the side of your mat and your arms and shoulders should be one long straight line from finger tips to finger tips. Don't let your back shoulder roll forward. Make sure that your forward knee is still directly over your ankle and facing straight forward, not turning inwards.
- Look over the middle finger of your forward hand. (If you have neck problems, look at the side of the room). Reach with your arms, expand your chest, and roll both your front and back thighs to the outside, opening your hips. Breathe.

Reverse Warrior – left side *(Urdhva Virabhadrasana II)*

Fig 47

- Inhale your forward palm up and exhale your forward arm up, over your head, and back in one big arc while lowering your back hand to your back leg **Fig 47**. Keep your forward knee over your ankle and turned out. Keep your back leg straight. Make sure that both feet are still flat on the floor.
- Look at the ceiling with a long neck. (If you have neck problems, look forward). Breathe.

Side Warrior – left side *(Virabhadrasana II)*

Fig 46A
Inhale back to Side Warrior.

Extended side angle – left side *(Utthita Parsvakonasana)*

Fig 48

- Exhale as you reach forward with your front arm, keeping your feet and legs in the **Side Warrior** position, and your front knee directly over your front ankle.
- Lower your front elbow to your front knee as you inhale your back arm in a big arc up, over your head, and forward with palm facing down.
- Look up at the ceiling under your outstretched arm, keeping the back of your neck long **Fig 48**. (If you have neck problems, look to the side of the room). Make one long straight line from the edge of your back foot to your outstretched finger tips. Keep your front knee turned out and your upper shoulder rolled back. Don't let the lower side of your torso collapse. Breathe. (For Level II add Fig 50, Level III add Fig 51)
- Inhale back to **Side Warrior,** exhale to **Lunge,** inhale to **High Plank,** exhale to **Low Plank,** inhale to **Up dog,** exhale to **Down dog**, look forward, step your left foot forward, and complete the entire **Side Warrior Sequence** on the other side, exhale to **Lunge,** inhale **to High Plank,** exhale to **Low Plank,** inhale to **Up dog,** exhale to **Down dog** (take a couple deep breaths here if you want).
- Look forward and jump your feet between your hands
- Exhale to **Forward bend,** grab your big toes with your index and middle fingers, angle your elbows out, and relax **Fig 49**. Breathe. You should feel your hamstrings gently stretching, but no stress on your lower back. If you feel lower back stress, soften your knees.
- Inhale as you slowly roll up to **Mountain** one vertebra at a time.

Fig 49

Level II hand to floor Extended side angle – left side *(Utthita Parsvakonasana)*

Fig 50

- This pose is the same as **Extended side angle** except that you lower your front arm from your knee to the floor with your hand next to the big toe of your forward foot, fingers facing the same direction as your toes **Fig 50**. Use a block for your hand if you want.
- Keep your hips lowered to maintain a long straight line from the outside edge of your back foot to the finger tips of your upper hand. Breathe. Many teachers teach this pose with the front arm on the outside of the front leg instead of on the inside. The problem with this is that as you roll your upper shoulder back, you either push your front knee in with your lower arm or you must lean back (sway back) from your lower back. This is bad for your knees or your lower back.
- If you want more intensity than you get with your arm on the inside, **Bound side angle Fig 51** is a better alternative. Continue from **Extended side angle.**

Level III Bound side angle - right side *(Baddha Utthita Parsvakonasana)*

Fig 51

Fig 51A

- **Bound side angle Fig 51** is the same as **Extended side angle** except that you reach your lower arm back under your forward leg, lower your upper arm down behind, and grab your fingers behind your back **Fig 51A**. Your upper arm palm should be facing away from your back and your lower arm palm should be facing towards your back.
- Roll your upper shoulder back, make a straight line from the outside edge of your back foot to the top of your head, and open your chest. Breathe.
- Continue from **Extended side angle.**

In fifth sun salutation:

Forward Facing Warrior Sequence

This sequence stretches and strengthens chest and lungs, shoulders and neck, abdomen and groins, arms, back muscles, thighs, calves, and ankles. It also improves balance, posture, and endurance.

Forward facing warrior or Warrior I – left side *(Virabhadrasana I)*

Fig 52

Fig 52A

Fig 52B

- From **Down dog,** look forward and inhale your right foot next to your right hand. (The left side is pictured.) Keep your hips down, your back leg and spine straight, and your right knee directly over your right ankle. You may turn your back foot to 45 degrees **Fig 52A** or stay on the ball of your back foot **Fig 52B**. (If this is too difficult, lower your back knee to the floor **Fig 52**). Whichever variation you choose, your back foot should be hip width from your front foot and your hips squared facing straight forward. Many teachers recommend that your back foot should be aligned directly behind your front foot instead of hip width in this pose. The problem with this is that most people cannot square their hips without twisting their lower back in this position. It is often dangerous for your lower back to twist it and then do a back bend.
- Extend your arms straight forward with your biceps next to your ears and your palms facing each other. Stretch long from your tailbone to your finger tips.
- Inhale your torso up to perpendicular keeping your biceps next to your ears. (If you have lower back problems or this is too difficult, you can inhale up to standing and then lower your hips). Look forward.
- Lower your hips as you lift your ears. Relax your shoulders as you send energy up your extended arms. Keep your biceps next to your ears. Breathe. (For Level II add Fig 54.)
- Continue by exhaling to **Lunge,** inhaling to **High plank,** exhaling to **Low plank,** inhaling to **Up dog,** exhaling to **Down dog** inhaling your left foot forward for the **Forward facing warrior sequence.** Exhale to **Lunge,** inhale to **High plank,** exhale to **Low plank,** inhale to **Up dog,** exhale to **Down dog,** (take several deep breaths here if you want).
- Look forward and jump your feet between your hands, exhale to **Forward bend,** step on your hands, palms facing up **Fig 53**. The backs of your hands should be flat on the floor with your toes touching your wrists. Relax your neck. Breathe. You should feel your hamstrings gently stretching, but no stress on your lower back. If you feel lower back stress, soften your knees.
- Inhale as you slowly roll up to **Mountain** one vertebra at a time.

Fig 53

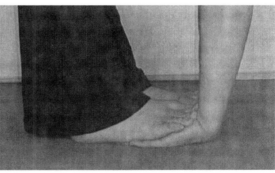

Fig 53A

Level II Balance warrior or Warrior III - left side *(Virabhadrasana III)*

Fig 54

- From **Forward facing warrior,** inhale to standing on your front leg with extended arms and biceps next to your ears. Your back leg should be straight with your foot slightly off the floor. Your front foot and knee should be facing forward. Reach long from your finger tips to the ball of your back foot. Lift your front knee and thigh, but don't lock your knee.
- Exhale as you slowly bend forward from your hips, not your waist **Fig 54**. Keeping that long straight line from your finger tips to the ball of your back foot, make sure that your hips stay level. If balancing is too difficult, you can extend your arms to your sides like airplane wings or use a wall to help balance. Although the full pose makes a letter "T", go only as far as you can maintain both your diaphragmatic breathing and your form.
- Reach in both directions. Breathe.
- Continue by inhaling back to **Forward facing warrior.**

Standing Forward Bend Sequence

This sequence stretches hamstrings, inner leg muscles, spine, and wrists. It strengthens legs and back, and opens your shoulders and chest. It improves blood circulation to the head and brain, stimulates your glandular systems, and improves posture, balance, and digestion.

Intense Side Stretch A *(Parsvottanasana A)*

Fig 55   Fig 56

- From **Mountain,** exhale your right foot about 3 feet back, front foot facing forward, back foot slightly angled, feet hip width apart, and hips squared facing forward.
- Inhale your arms overhead with straight arms, palms touching, and thumbs crossed **Fig 55**.
- Keeping both legs and arms straight, but not locked, slowly curl forward as you exhale until your forehead touches your front knee **Fig 56**. Go only as far as you can without any strain on your lower back.
- Touch your fingertips to the floor in front of your foot. (If you need to separate your hands for balance, do so). Breathe.

Intense Side Stretch B *(Parsvottanasana B)*

Fig 57   **Fig 58**

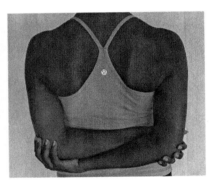

Fig 59   **Fig 59A**

- Inhale back to standing and exhale your arms behind you into prayer hands **Fig 59**. (If you cannot make prayer hands behind yourself, grab your elbows or forearms **Fig 59A**). Roll your shoulders back and extend your elbows back. Keep both legs straight.
- Inhale, standing tall and straight **Fig 57.**
- Exhale folding forward from your hips with a long straight spine until your chin touches your shin. **Fig 58.** Breathe.
- Inhale back to standing and step your right foot forward, your left foot back, and repeat both **Intense side stretch A & B** on the other side.

Wide standing forward bend A *(Prasarita Padottanasana A)*

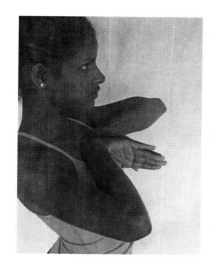

Fig 60

Fig 61

Fig 62

- Exhale your left foot wide (4-5 feet) with your toes and body facing the side of your mat. Make sure that your heels are slightly wider than your toes.
- Inhale the back of your hands together next to the center of your chest, with wrists, back of your hands, and fingers touching **Fig 60**. Your elbows will be facing forward.
- Exhale your arms long, keeping the backs of your hands together, and stretching your elbows **Fig 61**.
- Inhale your arms back behind your back and exhale as you interlace your fingers.
- Inhale your interlaced fingers up, keeping your back straight, and knees and thighs lifted.

- Slowly exhale to a forward fold, keeping your abdomen, arms, knees, and thighs lifted, and your spine long and straight. Bend from the hips, not the waist.
- Touch the top of your head to the floor **Fig 62**. If it doesn't touch the floor, that's OK; just go in that direction. Feel the inner legs and hamstrings stretching. You should not feel any type of discomfort in your lower back. Breathe.
- Release your hands and exhale them to the floor.

Straddle fold twist

Fig 63

- Place your left hand in front of your face, fingers facing right, and inhale while straightening your left arm. Keep a long straight back.
- Put your right hand to your right hip and roll your right shoulder back with an exhale.
- Inhale your right arm straight up and look at your thumb **Fig 63**. (If you have neck problems, look at the side of the room). Keep both arms and legs straight, but not locked. Try to make one straight line from hand to hand, shoulders included. Breathe.
- Exhale down and repeat with your right hand on the floor facing left. Breathe.

Wide standing forward bend B *(Prasarita Padottanasana B)*

- With both hands shoulder width apart, fingers facing forward, and elbows facing straight back, exhale folding forward with a long straight spine until the top of your head touches the floor **Fig 64**.
- Keep your knees and thighs lifted. Do not support your weight with your head. Breathe.
- When you are ready, walk your feet closer together, put your hands on your hips, lift your abdomen and knees, and inhale up to standing. Step to **Mountain** at the front of your mat.

Fig 64

Balancing Sequence

These poses will strengthen your legs and spine, open your hips, stretch your back, and build overall strength and stamina. They are good for sciatica and lower back problems, and improve balance and concentration. Use a wall as a prop to help your balance when you first begin if necessary. As you start each balancing pose, feel your balancing foot on the floor as though it had four wheels, two in the front and two in the back. Lift your toes and spread them, then relax them. Stand tall in each pose.

Balanced leg extension (bent knee)

Fig 65   **Fig 66**

Level II Balanced leg extension (straight leg)
(Utthita Hasta Padangusthasana)

Fig 65A   **Fig 66A**

Fig 65B   **Fig 66B**

- From **Mountain,** with your right hand on your right hip, lift your left leg with a bent knee, and hold your left knee with your left hand **Fig 65**.
- For Level II, after lifting your left leg, wrap your first two fingers around your big toe, and straighten your left leg **Fig 65B**. (You may wrap a strap around your left foot if necessary **Fig 65A**.)
- Keeping your standing leg straight without locking the knee, extend your right arm to your right side as you extend your left leg to your left side **Fig 68**.
- Keep your right knee bent or for Level II keep it straight **Fig 66A, 66B**.
- Stand tall. Open your shoulders, chest, and hips. Look forward. Breathe.
- Repeat on the other side.

Flamingo

Fig 67

Level II Dancer *(Natarajasana I)*

Fig 68

- From **Mountain**, inhale both arms over your head.
- Exhale your right hand down as you lift your right foot behind yourself.
- Grab the inside of your right foot with your right hand. Keep your left arm and leg extended **Fig 67.** Stand tall. Breathe.
- For Level II, bend forward from the hips, reaching long with your left arm, and lifting your right knee as high as possible **Fig 68**. The more you reach forward and kick back at the same time, the better you can balance. Make sure that your upper leg does not angle outwards. Focus your eyes straight ahead on something that doesn't move. Breathe.
- Repeat on the other side.

Dancing Shiva (bent knee) Level II (straight leg)
(Natarajasana II)

Fig 69   **Fig 69A**

- From **Mountain**, with a long straight spine, keep your left foot facing straight forward as you exhale and lift your right knee up, placing your left hand on the outside of your right knee **Fig 69**.
- For Level II, hold the outside of your right foot with your left hand and extend your leg straight **Fig 69A**.
- Inhale as you extend your right arm to shoulder height (palm vertical) and exhale as you slowly turn your torso, right arm, and head to the right and look past your right hand. (If you have neck problems, look forward). Breathe.
- Repeat on the other side.

Level III Eagle *(Garudasana)*

Fig 70   **Fig 70A**

- From **Mountain**, lower your hips and lift your left leg up and over your right leg above the knee, balancing on your right foot.
- Hook your left foot behind your right calf with your toes on the left side, facing down and forward.
- Place your right elbow in the crook of your left elbow and bring the palms of your hands together.
- Interlace your fingers **Fig 70A** or make prayer hands **Fig 70**. Look forward. Breathe.
- Repeat on the other side.

Tip toe balance

Fig 71

Fig 72

Fig 73

- From **Mountain**, with your feet hip width apart and toes facing straight ahead, lift your arms straight forward with your palms facing the floor.
- Stand up as tall as possible on your tip toes with a straight back, looking forward. Broaden your shoulders and the sides of your chest **Fig 71**.
- Slowly lower your hips as you bend your knees. Stay on your tip toes and keep a straight back. Keep breathing as you lower your hips to just slightly higher than your knees **Fig 72**. (Don't do the knee bend part of this pose if you have knee problems).
- With a straight back and staying on your tip toes, slowly stand back up and see how tall you can get. Continue to breathe.
- Stay on your tip toes and bring your hands to prayer hands with thumbs touching the center of your chest. Keeping your feet and hips facing straight forward and your thumbs touching the center of your chest, exhale as you turn your torso, then head to your right side **Fig 73**. (If you have neck problems, don't twist your neck.) Breathe.
- Inhale to center and exhale to your left side. Breathe.
- Inhale to center and relax back to **Mountain**.

Level II Balancing hip opener

Fig 74

- From **Mountain**, lift your left ankle and place it on your right leg just above the knee.
- Interlace your fingers behind your back, open your chest and lower your hips as you bend forward. Try to touch your chest to your left leg and sit your hips down as far as possible.
- Lift your hands as high as possible **Fig 74**. Look at the floor. Breathe.
- Inhale back to standing and repeat on the other side.

Tree *(Vrksasana)*

Fig 75   **Fig 75A**

Fig 75B   **Fig 75C**

- From **Mountain**, place the sole of your right foot on the inside of your left leg somewhere between the ankle and the top of the thigh, above or below the knee. Lift the knee and thigh of your standing leg as you lift your abdomen in and up. Roll the bent knee back, opening your hip as you make prayer hands at the center of your chest **Fig 75**.
- Keeping your hands in prayer position, lift them straight up until your arms are straight, without locking your elbows **Fig 75A-C**. Relax your shoulders and stand tall. Open your chest and hips. Look straight forward and breathe.
- Repeat on the other side.

Transition/re-aligning

Squat *(Malasana)*

Fig 76

• From **Mountain**, with your feet facing straight forward about one and one half feet apart, and your arms forward with palms touching, lower your hips as low as possible without lifting your heels **Fig 76**. If this is too easy, interlace your fingers behind yourself and lift your hands. If you cannot get your heels down, try a wedge under your heels. Breathe.

Level III Crane (*Bakasana*)

Fig 77

- From **Squat**, place your hands on the floor shoulder width apart with your fingers facing forward. Your palms should be flat on the floor with your fingers spread. Your triceps should support the inside of your knees.
- Slowly move your weight forward and gently lift one foot.
- Once you are balanced, keep that foot up as you slowly go to only the big toe of the other foot on the floor.
- If you are comfortable in this position, gently lift your toe and balance on your hands **Fig 77**. Look at the floor. Breathe. Do not try this pose if you have wrist problems or a weak upper body. If you feel that you are losing your balance or your arms are giving out, roll one shoulder down and roll to your side on the floor.
- Once you can balance for about 20 seconds, try to straighten your arms **Fig 77A**.

Fig 77A

Back Strengthening Sequence

These poses are important to keep the back strong and flexible. They build core strength while stretching and strengthening the spine, buttocks, abdomen, chest, thighs, and shoulders. They relieve stress and improve posture and are great for sciatica and lower back problems as well as asthma. For many people with lower back pain, doing **Cobra** (Fig 78) pose (four breaths) followed by **Child** (Fig 82) pose (eight breaths) can often relieve the pain. Do several repetitions and end with **Lying spinal twist** (Fig 105-106) on both sides.

Cobra *(Bhujangasana)*

Fig 78

- Lying flat on your stomach on your mat with knees and feet together, place your hands under your shoulders with your fingers facing forward.
- As you inhale, peel your upper body off the floor, keeping your belly button on the floor and your elbows close to your body **Fig 78**. Make as much room as possible between your shoulders and your ears. Make sure that you are holding yourself up with your back and not your arms. Look forward. Breathe.
- Exhale flat on your stomach with your arms at your sides, palms facing up, and your left ear on the mat.

Lying boat and locust *(Salabhasana)*

Fig 79

Fig 80

- Lying flat on your stomach with your arms at your sides, inhale your arms as far forward as possible with palms facing.
- Inhale and lift your arms, upper torso, and legs away from the floor **Fig 79**. Reach long and look down. Breathe.
- Inhale your arms up and back as you lift your torso and legs higher **Fig 80**. Lift high and look forward. Breathe.
- Exhale flat on your stomach with your arms at your sides, palms facing up, and your right ear on the mat.

Bow *(Dhanurasana)*

Fig 81

- Lying flat on your stomach with your arms at your sides, bend your knees and take hold of your ankles with your hands. Keep your knees hip width apart.
- Inhale and lift your heels away from your seat, lifting your thighs off the floor. Your upper torso and head will also lift off the floor **Fig 81**. Make space between your shoulders and your ears. Look forward. Breathe.
- Follow with **Child**.

Transition/re-aligning

Child (*Balasana*)

Fig 82

- Lying on your stomach, place your bent knees to the sides of your mat as you move your hips back, sitting on your feet with the palms of your hands on the floor **Fig 82**. Your torso should be resting between your thighs. Big toes should be touching, arms should be extended, and your forehead should be on the floor. Feel your lower back extending and releasing. Relax. Breathe into your lower back.

Cobbler *(Baddha Konasana)*

Fig 83   **Fig 83A**

- Sitting tall, bring the soles of your feet t ogether with your heels close to your pelvis.
- Hold your feet or big toes with your hands.
- Lower your knees towards the floor. Do not force your knees down or round your back **Fig 83**. Breathe.

Abs Sequence

These poses target the abs and will build core strength. Strong abs support the alignment of the spine and the abdominal organs.

Leg lifts *(Urdhva Prasarita Padasana)*

Fig 84

Fig 85

Fig 86

Fig 87

- Reclining on your elbows with your hands under your buttocks (palms down), extend both legs and lift your feet about 4 inches off the floor **Fig 84**. Keep your lower abdomen flat. Breathe.
- After 30 seconds to a minute, slowly lift your straight legs to perpendicular **Fig 85** and then lower them as slowly as possible **Fig 86, 87**. Keep breathing.
- Repeat as many times as you want. Keep your legs long and your neck relaxed. Do not touch your heels to the floor.
- Lift your right leg to perpendicular keeping your left heel 4 inches off the floor.
- Slowly lower your right leg without touching the floor and repeat with your left leg. Breathe. Relax.

Level II Boat *(Navasana)*

Fig 88

- Lying flat on your back with extended legs and arms at your sides, simultaneously lift your torso and your legs (with bent knees) off the floor.
- Hold the back of your knees with your hands and balance on your sitting bones and tailbone. Make sure that you are not rounding your back
- Let go of your knees and straighten your arms **Fig 88**. Keep your spine long from your tailbone to the top of your head. If you can straighten your legs, do so. Extend the back of your neck and broaden your chest and shoulders. Look forward. Breathe.

Level III Boat sit-ups

Fig 89

Fig 90

- Lay on your back with arms, legs, and head lifted **Fig 89**.
- Exhale your upper body and legs up to **Boat, Fig 90.**
- Inhale as you slowly release and repeat several times. Keep your spine, arms, and legs straight. Bend from the hips, not the lower back. Breathe.

Floor eagle *(Supta Garudasana)*

Fig 91

- Lying flat on your back, lift your right leg over your left leg and tuck your right toes behind your left calf.

- Place your right elbow in the crook of your left elbow and bring the palms of your hands together.
- Interlace your fingers or make prayer hands.
- Lift your shoulders and tailbone off the floor. Pull your abdomen against your spine **Fig 91**. Hold and breathe.
- Repeat with the other side.
- Release and extend your arms straight back above your head as you extend your legs and inhale.
- Grab your knees with your hands and squeeze before rolling up to sitting.

Seated Forward Bend Sequence

These poses have a calming effect while stretching the hamstrings, spine, and shoulders. They stimulate digestion and relieve mild depression, anxiety, and insomnia. Be very careful of your lower back in these poses. You should feel your hamstrings stretching but never any tension in your lower back. Tight hamstrings are a frequent cause of lower back problems because when your hamstrings won't stretch any farther, the entire force in bending forward is centered in your lower back. Since your lower back is then the fulcrum, the pressure on it is multiplied many times. If you cannot touch your toes, use a strap. If these poses are difficult for you, try elevating your hips by sitting on a folded blanket.

Seated forward bend *(Paschimottanasana)*

Fig 92

- Seated on the floor with your legs extended in front of you, tilt your pelvis so that your lower pelvis is as far back as possible and your upper pelvis is as far forward as possible. Sit up tall.
- Grab your feet or use a strap around them. Be extremely aware and careful of your lower back and don't forcefully pull yourself into the forward bend.
- Lengthen your front torso, extend your back, and keep your neck in a straight line with your spine as you lengthen forward. Bend forward from your hips, not your waist. Go slowly.
- First touch your abdomen to your thighs, then your chest **Fig 92**. Take your time. With every inhale stretch longer and with every exhale soften slightly deeper. Breathe.
- Inhale as you slowly come out of this pose.

Separate side arch *(Parivrtta Janu Sirsasana)*

Fig 93

- Seated on the floor with your legs extended in front of you, bend your right knee so that your right foot touches the inside of your left thigh. Lower your right knee and open your hips, but do not force. Sit up tall.
- Exhale as you grab your left big toe with the index and middle finger of your left hand (or use a strap) and make a straight line from your left hand to the fingers of your right hand, keeping your right shoulder rolled back.
- Inhale your right arm over in one big arc, keeping your shoulders and arms aligned. Your left elbow should be on the inside of your left knee. Look at the ceiling **Fig 93**. (If you have neck problems, look to the side of the room). Breathe.
- Inhale as you slowly come out of this pose.
- Continue with **Separate leg head to knee Fig 94 or 95** on this side and then repeat both on the other side.

Separate leg head to knee *(Janu Sirsasana)*

Fig 94

- From **Separate side** arch, face your torso towards your left foot.
- Inhale and extend your arms up, interlacing your fingers.
- Use a strap or reach your interlaced fingers around your left foot. Do not pull yourself into the forward bend with your hands or the strap.
- Option 1 **Fig 94**: Exhale as you bend forward from the hips, keeping your back long and straight. Keep your front torso lifted and be very careful with your lower back. Feel your hamstrings stretching, not your lower back. Your abdomen, then your chest, and then your face should make contact with your legs.

Fig 95

- Option 2 **Fig 95**: On your exhale, slowly curl from sitting up straight, down to forehead to knee. Make sure that there is absolutely no strain to your lower back and that your entire back, from the tip of your tailbone to the top of your head, is rounded. This option will stretch your back more than your hamstrings. Breathe.
- Repeat **Separate side arch,** then **Separate leg head to knee** on the other side.

Transition/re-aligning

Pigeon A *(Kapotasana A)*

Fig 96

- From **Separate leg head to knee** without moving your right leg, slide your left leg around straight behind you so that you are resting on the top of the left thigh, top of the left foot and the outside of the bent right leg. If you have healthy knees, make sure that your right knee is as far to the right as possible and your right foot is as far forward as possible. If you have knee problems, keep your right knee facing more forward and your right foot farther back.
- Allow gravity to lower your hips. Walk your hands back as far as you can, roll your shoulders back, and lift and expand your chest **Fig 96**. Lengthen your arms. Make space between your shoulders and your ears. Lengthen your spine. (If you have lower back problems, be very attentive to your lower back). Look forward. Breathe.
- Continue with **Pigeon B** before repeating on the other side.

Pigeon B *(Kapotasana B)*

Fig 97

- From **Pigeon A** without moving your legs, walk your hands forward and rest on your elbows. (Shown with right leg back) Breathe.
- If this is comfortable, walk your hands out farther until your arms are extended with the palms of your hands shoulder width and flat on the floor **Fig 97**. Breathe.
- Continue with **High plank,** and then repeat **Pigeon A & B** on the other side.

Back Bend Sequence

This sequence will stretch the front of the body, your chest, neck, throat, spine, and lungs. It will strengthen your entire back and stimulate abdominal organs, thyroid, and pituitary. It is good for asthma, back pain, and high blood pressure and reduces anxiety, fatigue, depression, backache, headache, and insomnia. Make sure that you protect your lower back by bending evenly along the entire spine with a lifted chest and ribs, so that the upper body takes more of the bend and you don't hinge at your lower back.

Camel *(Ustrasana)*

Fig 98

- Kneel with your knees hip width apart and your hips directly above your knees. If your knees hurt in this position, you can fold your mat, making it thicker.

- Place the palms of your hands on your lower back with your fingers touching your buttocks and your thumbs facing out.
- Roll your shoulders back and bring your elbows closer together.
- Tuck your tailbone and slowly curve backwards, lifting your ribs. Feel as thought you are resting your spine over a ball. Do not let your lower back collapse. Extend your spine.
- Lower one hand, then the other to your heels **Fig 98**. If you need to, turn your toes under to elevate your heels. If you still can't reach your feet, continue in the pose with your hands supporting your lower back. Open your chest and lift your sternum (breastbone). Look up, without letting the back of your neck collapse. Find a balance between forcefully holding your neck up and letting it fall back. Keep your hips directly above your knees. Breathe.

Bridge (*Setu Bandha Sarvangasana*)

Fig 99

- Lying on your back, bend your knees so that your feet are hip width apart near your seat. Face your feet straight forward. Your arms are at your sides.
- Pushing down on your feet and arms, do a pelvic tilt and begin to slowly lift your tailbone off the floor, keeping your knees and feet parallel and the back of your neck long. Lift one vertebra at a time off the floor, keeping your tailbone tucked to protect your lower back.
- Once your seat is lifted several inches, bring your hands together with interlaced fingers and roll your upper arms under your shoulders, keeping your arms straight and on the floor.
- Continue to tuck your tailbone and lift your hips until your thighs are parallel with the floor **Fig 99**. Be careful with your neck and your lower back. Breathe.

Level II Bridge (straight legs)

Fig 100   **Fig 101**

- In **Bridge**, bring your hands to your lower back with your fingers facing out. Straighten your legs and bring your feet flat on the floor **Fig 100.**
- You may extend one leg at a time perpendicular in this pose if you want **Fig 101**. Breathe.

Level III Wheel *(Urdhva Dhanurasana)*

Fig 102

- Lying on your back, bend your knees so that your feet are hip width apart near your seat. Face your feet straight forward. Place your hands (palms down) shoulder width apart next to your head with your fingers facing your shoulders.
- Keeping your knees hip width apart and your elbows shoulder width apart, press down with your feet and hands as you lift your hips.
- Straighten your arms **Fig 102** (you may rest half way up on the top of your head). Do not let your feet splay out as this is hard on your lower back. Keep your tailbone slightly tucked and relax your neck, looking straight ahead or down at the floor. Breathe. Come out of wheel slowly and with control.

Transition/re-aligning

Cat/Cow *(Bidalasana)*

Fig 103　　　　　　Fig 104

- Standing on your hands and knees, exhale and lift the middle of your back as you tuck your tailbone and extend the back of your neck, looking at your knees. Lift your abdomen in and up **Fig 103**. Your spine should look like the upper half of a circle or a cat with its back up.
- Inhale your head up, tilt your pelvis the other way and lower the middle of your back, looking forward **Fig 104**. Your spine should look like the lower half of a circle.
- Repeat several times.

Child (optional) Fig 82

Hip Opener/Twist Sequence

Besides cooling you down at the end of your session, these poses stretch your spine, shoulders and hips while relieving stress, lower back pain, and sciatica. They are important for re-aligning and releasing your spine after the **Back Bend sequence**, improve digestion and help asthma and high blood pressure.

Lying bent knee stretch *(Ardha Pavanamuktasana)*

Fig 105

- Lying flat on your back on your mat, bend your left knee.
- Interlace your fingers, place your hands below your bent knee, and pull it towards your left armpit. Keep your back and head flat on your mat and your right calf on the floor **Fig 105**. If your right calf doesn't touch the floor, flex your right foot. Breathe.
- Continue with **Lying spinal twist**.

Lying spinal twist *(Supta Matsyendrasana)*

Fig 106

- From **Lying bent knee stretch,** extend your left arm, palm facing down.
- Place the palm of your right hand on the outside of your left knee and slowly exhale your bent left knee over to your right side. Keep your right leg straight and your left shoulder on the floor. Your left foot should be resting on the side of your right knee **Fig 106**. Do not push your left knee to the floor, let gravity slowly bring it to the floor. Release and relax. Breathe.
- Continue with **Lying bent knee stretch** and **Lying spinal twist** on the other side.

Lying extended leg A & B *(Supta Padangusthasana)*

Fig 107

Fig 108

Fig 107A

Fig 108A

- Lying flat on your back with both knees bent, straighten your right leg as you grab your left big toe with your left index and fore fingers **Fig 107A** or lasso your left foot with a strap **Fig 107** and hold it with your left hand.

- Extend your right arm out to the side. Straighten your left leg up and your right leg straight on the floor with your calf touching. Keep your head and shoulders on the floor.
- Slowly lower your left leg to the left, keeping both hips and both shoulders on the floor **Fig 108 or 108A**. Keep both legs straight without locking your knees. Open your hips; open your shoulders; open your chest; open the entire front of your body. Breathe.
- Repeat on the other side.

Rock the baby *(Akarna Dhanurasana)*

Fig 109

- Sitting with your legs extended in front on you, cross your right leg so that your right ankle rests on top of your left knee.
- Place the sole of your right foot on the inside of your left elbow.
- Reach your right arm around to outside of your right knee and interlace your fingers.
- Sit up tall and straight and hug your leg to your torso **Fig 109**. Breathe.
- Repeat on the other side.

Sitting twist (*Ardha Matsyendrasana*)

Fig 110A

Fig 110B

Fig 110

- Sitting with your legs bent in front of you, bend your left knee until your left foot touches your seat.
- Place your right foot on the left side of your left knee. Your right knee will now point towards the ceiling. Sit up as tall as you can.
- Place your right hand next to your tailbone, fingers facing away.
- Wrap your left arm around your right knee and hug your thigh to your torso.
- Inhale tall. Exhale your abdomen to the right. Inhale tall. Exhale your chest to the right. Inhale tall. Exhale your shoulders to the right. Inhale tall. Exhale and look to the rear **Fig 110** (If you have neck problems, look to the side of the room **Fig110A**). Breathe.
- Repeat on the other side.

Relaxing Sequence

This important sequence should not be omitted. It helps your body integrate the benefits of your session and relaxes your body/mind, preparing you for the rest of your day. As you totally relax every muscle and let go of all your internal tension, keep your mind relaxed, yet alert.

Corpse *(Savasana)*

Fig 111

- Start **Corpse pose** by lying flat on your back on your mat. Your arms should be at your sides with your palms facing up and your feet should be hip width apart.
- Close your eyes and melt into your mat **Fig 111**. Let any tension from your Yoga session, your day, your job or school, or even your childhood go. Slowly erase everything on the blackboard. Do not think about what you did earlier or what you need to do later.
- Observe your body right now. Relax. Let go. Release. Start slow, relaxed, even abdominal breathing.

Breathing A – Short inhale, long exhale - 1:2

As you continue in **Corpse pose** with eyes closed, start abdominal breathing counting 3 seconds for each inhale and 6 seconds for each exhale. Keep your breath flowing smoothly in and out and feel as though you are filling your abdomen with air with each inhale. Do not force. Mentally follow your breath and feel the increasing sense of calm with each exhale. Once 3 in and 6 out can be done smoothly without stress or lightheadedness, try 4 seconds inhale and 8 seconds exhale. Do eight repetitions. Do not exceed 4:8 seconds or eight repetitions. After the eighth exhale, breathe normally and continue with **Guided relaxation**. **Short inhale/long exhale** breathing has a beneficial effect on the autonomic nervous system, slows the heart rate, is therapeutic for asthma, encourages relaxation, and decreases the amount of air remaining in your lungs after exhalation. It is a great preparation for final relaxation.

Breathing B – Retention *(Kumbhaka)* - 1:1:1:1 (Level II)

Instead of **Breathing A**, you can also practice **Breathing B.** Rather than practicing both in the same session, alternate between them. At the end of each inhalation or exhalation, the breath naturally stops, just for a moment, before you continue. **Retention** breathing is consciously extending these pauses. Start with abdominal breathing in **Corpse** with closed eyes. To begin, inhale for 4 seconds, hold for 4 seconds and exhale for 4 seconds and repeat several times. Practice until this is smooth. Do not cork your breath while holding. Once this is smooth, inhale for 4 seconds, exhale for 4 seconds and hold for 4 seconds and repeat several times. As soon as you can do both smoothly without stress or roughness, you are ready to put it all together and practice **Retention** breathing. Inhale 4 seconds, hold 4 seconds, exhale 4 seconds, hold 4 seconds and repeat. Do a total of 4 repetitions. Do not exceed 4 seconds for each action or 4 cycles. After the fourth cycle, breathe normally and continue with **Guided relaxation**. **Retention** breathing increases the blood's capacity to hold CO_2 and promotes concentration and relaxation.

Guided relaxation

Lying on your back in **Corpse** with eyes closed, consciously relax your toes, feet, heels, ankles, shins, calves, knees, thighs, hamstrings, hips, tailbone, lower back, abdomen, upper back, chest, finger tips, fingers, hands, thumbs, wrists, forearms, elbows, biceps, triceps, shoulders, the back of your neck, throat, jaw, tongue, lips, the back of your head, crown of your head, forehead, eyebrows, eyelids, eyes, and mind. Remain in this relaxed position for a minimum of several minutes and a maximum of about fifteen minutes. Do not suppress or hold on to thoughts. If thoughts arise, let them come and go like the bubbles in a glass of soda or champagne; appearing at the bottom out of nowhere, traveling to the top and disappearing again. When you are ready, roll over to your right side and slowly push yourself up to sitting. Remain sitting with your eyes open until you feel that you are ready to get up. (If you go from deep relaxation to standing too fast, you could pass out). Bring this happy relaxed state with you whatever you do next.

Sequencing

You may, of course, follow this entire session as presented. You may also specialize in different sequences on different days, doing some sequences one day and others the next. Some days you may want an intense workout and some days a restorative session. You can flow from pose to pose holding each for only a couple breaths or you may hold each for a longer period of time. You may want to select fewer poses and do each pose or sequence twice or combine both of the Warrior series into one big series for greater strength and endurance. (Side Warrior, Forward Facing Warrior, Balance Warrior, Forward Facing Warrior, Side Warrior, Reverse Warrior, Side Warrior, Extended Side Angle, Side Warrior and possibly repeat before Lunge, High Plank, Low Plank, Up Dog, Down Dog, Lunge and the entire sequence on the other side.) Once you are confident in the entire set of poses, you can begin to experiment. There are thousands of different Yoga poses and I have only presented a basic sampling, although you probably won't really need any more than these. There are some general rules for sequencing: get your muscles warmed up before starting deeper or more difficult poses; always do both sides of your body; start with a less extreme pose of one type, followed by more extreme poses of that type, followed by a less extreme pose for re-alignment; don't follow an extreme back bend with an extreme forward bend; do follow back bends with gentle forward bends or twists; don't just do the poses that you are good at and omit the poses that are difficult for you; always end with relaxation. Every Yoga session should start with breathing, build up heat and intensity, and then include deep stretching as you cool down to relaxation. Go slowly; your body will thank you.

Partner Yoga

PY1   **PY2**   **PY3**

Yoga poses can also be done together with a partner. The possibilities for Partner Yoga are extensive and beyond the scope of this book. There are many good books on this subject available. Besides being fun, Partner Yoga is a great way to coordinate and balance your control and surrender, strength and flexibility, and other opposites with a partner. (see PY 1-3)

Anywhere Yoga

Yoga can be done almost any time and anywhere. As you become more aware of your body, you will notice when it becomes tense or tight and you can stretch that area to relieve the tension. This is helpful while standing for long periods or when you must remain in the same position for an extended period of time. Some examples are: waiting in line or sightseeing (lower back tension), working at a computer or sitting at a desk (neck and shoulder tension), or any activity that is inactive or repetitive. Even simple stretches like pelvic tilts while standing and rolling your shoulders up, back, and down while sitting can relieve the tension. I am including Office, Shower, and Bed Yoga as examples. These aren't the only exercises nor the only times or places where a good stretch will relieve tension and re-vitalize your mind and body. We need to stretch throughout the day just like cats and dogs. You can use Yoga poses that you know or make up new ones. Be creative and listen to your body.

Office Yoga

OY1   OY2

OY3   OY4

OY5   OY6

I have included stretches for the wrists, neck and shoulders as well as a twist. These are excellent stretches for office workers and people who work with computers. You may need other stretches to relax parts of your body where your tension builds. We all have different bodies and we all retain stress slightly differently. (Although I have only shown these stretches on one side, you should stretch both sides of the body.) If you stretch and relieve both physical and mental tension every hour or as needed, you will do better work, have a better outlook, and feel refreshed. This will lower your stress level, give you more energy, regulate your blood pressure, enhance your immune system, and release endorphins. (see OY 1-6)

Shower Yoga

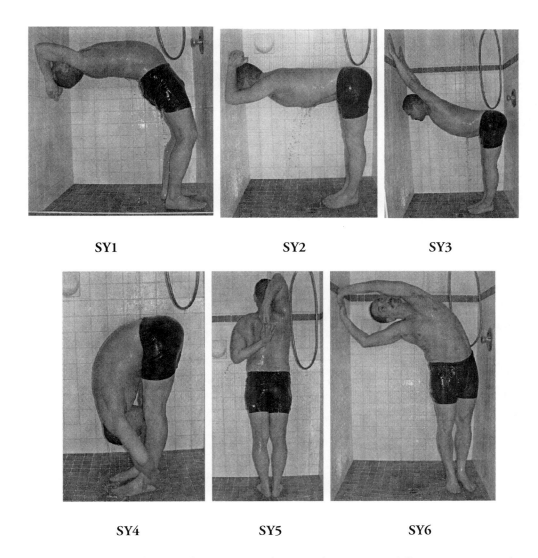

SY1   **SY2**   **SY3**

SY4   **SY5**   **SY6**

The shower is a great place to do some stretching in the morning. The warm water relaxes your muscles and the stretching stimulates your circulation. Since your muscles and joints are stiff in the morning from inactivity, this is an excellent way to get everything going. I am demonstrating mainly back stretches since I like to release a tight lower back in the morning, but you can do whichever poses work for you. Experiment and see what works best. (see SY1-6)

Bed Yoga

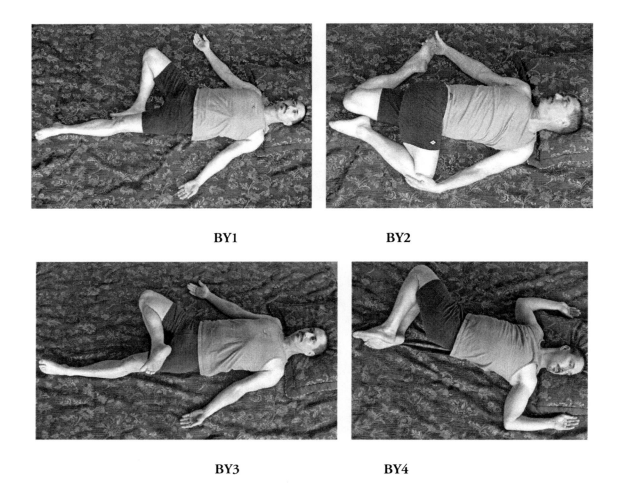

BY1   BY2

BY3   BY4

Bed is a great place to do some hip openers and twists. I do them before I go to sleep at night and between the first time my alarm goes off and when it's time to get up. Hold these poses for several minutes. Again, try some poses and see what works for you. (see BY1-4)

Quotes:

Ganga White

The most important purpose of Yoga is to bring about a deep transformation of the individual--an awakening of intelligence that is free of dependencies and romantic beliefs and ready to meet the accelerating challenges of the 21st century.

Erich Schiffmann

The purpose of Yoga is to facilitate the profound inner relaxation that accompanies fearlessness. The release from fear is what finally precipitates the full flowering of love.

J Krishnamurti

Intelligence comes into being when the mind, the heart, and the body are really harmonious.

Self-knowledge has no end – you don't come to an achievement, you don't come to a conclusion. It is an endless river. As one studies it, as one goes into it more and more, one finds peace.

One must know oneself as one is, not as one wishes to be, which is merely an ideal and therefore fictitious, unreal; it is only that which *is* that can be transformed, not that which you wish to be.

Albert Einstein

A man should look for what is, and not for what he thinks should be.

The following section contains various ideas or concepts that, like shoes, have been useful to me on my journey. If they fit you, they may also be useful on your own unique journey. Please feel free to try them on and see if they fit.

Belief and Identification

When you see through the filter of belief, you are filtering out everything that doesn't fit your beliefs. You are therefore unable to see with clarity and are viewing yourself and the world like the men in the story of the blind men and the elephant, where each blind man "sees" a totally different animal: the man who feels the tail (and filters out the rest) "sees" an elephant like a rope; the man who feels the trunk "sees" an elephant like a giant snake; and the man who feels the leg "sees" an elephant like a tree. The actual elephant is the sum of these and much more.

Beliefs separate us from each other and are a primary source of violence, war, and suffering. If you challenge my beliefs, I automatically react by defending those beliefs, creating conflict. This conflict is violence. Even if I don't react outwardly, my blood pressure rises, my pulse quickens, my breath becomes faster and shallower, and my entire body tenses and prepares for fight or flight. If you look at the many problem areas in the world, belief plays a major part. These conflicts are all fueled by the violence inherent in belief and this same violence takes place between us as individuals every day.

If we are chained down by beliefs, we do not have the freedom necessary to meet today's challenges with fresh, new solutions. We can only meet the new with the same old, static mind that is part of the problem. Since we and the world are both in a constant state of change, we cannot rely on static beliefs, no matter how valuable they were in the past. Don't let this idea become another belief. Use it as a working hypothesis.

A person who is free of beliefs solves the problems of life with working hypotheses which are viewed as temporary tools. Since he is not emotionally attached to these working hypotheses, he does not need to defend them and is free to see himself and his fellow beings directly, instead of through the distorting filter of belief.

Another distorting filter is identification. Many people not only identify themselves with a country, race, religion, political party, or profession but with sports teams, television shows, and even brand names of products. Whenever you identify yourself with something you are closing yourself off from everything else, building prison walls around yourself, reducing infinity to only what you know, and limiting your growth. Although the basic instinct for identification comes from our primitive tribal survival needs to identify with a tribe for mutual protection, we now live in another reality where identification more often leads to hate, racism, war, and even genocide. The security you seek from identification is an illusion based on fear. It is like cowering inside of a stone fortification instead of dancing out in the fresh air.

When I define myself as an American or Iranian, Caucasian or African, Christian or Buddhist, Republican or Democrat, capitalist or socialist, young or old, rich or poor, I am separating myself from others and viewing events, people, and my environment through a filter and can therefore never see clearly. You must see clearly to experience reality, that which actually *is*. Everything else is self-projection.

You can start to understand what actually *is* by observing, without belief or identification, comment or classification, condemnation or justification, what you perceive, think, feel, and do from moment to moment.

Creativity is new from moment to moment. It flows. It has no ambition, goals, purpose or motive.

Love is new from moment to moment. It also flows. It also has no ambition, goals, purpose or motive. When you start thinking about love, naming it, trying to hold on to it, it goes away. You cannot find love through effort. You can remove obstacles to love but you cannot make love happen.

By freeing your body of blockages, tensions, and residual stress, and your mind from beliefs and identifications, you let love and creativity happen.

You are the World

If we are violent, greedy and superficial, that is what we create, that is the society in which we live. Society is our relationship with each other. If you want to change society, you must start with yourself.

You are constantly changing and so is the world. There is no path to truth or reality, because the external world is constantly changing and so is your internal world. You can only have a path between two fixed places. You are not a fixed place. You are replacing most of the cells in your body on a regular basis and exchanging your body with the environment with every breath.

Following a path, a system, a "Master," an old book, or even the truth that you found yesterday is not Yoga. Real Yoga is finding your truth right now; being attentive to what *is* right now, not what "should be" or what someone else said, or what you said last week. Real Yoga is being in the present moment, being truly alive. Yoga is self-discovery. "Should be" doesn't allow the freedom necessary for self-discovery.

Competition and Comparison

People compare. People are competitive. When you are in a Yoga class and you compare your pose to the teacher's pose, or the person next to you, or some ideal that you saw in a book, or the pose you did yesterday, you are being human. We humans do that. The important thing is to neither pretend that you don't compare (because you do), or "try harder" so that your pose looks better in comparison (which is competition and focusing on the result instead of the process). The important thing is to simply observe. Once you see what is happening, without comment or condemnation, you are free to choose what you want to do about it, if anything. People are naturally competitive. Some people even compete to see who can be the most non-competitive! Comparison and competition are neither "good" nor "bad". They are tools that we can use, or if we are unaware, they can use us. Remember, Yoga is balance and balance is an active, ever-changing state. Just hold a balancing pose for a minute and see how balance is active and ever-changing, not passive and inert.

Internal and External Feedback

Although it is important to have one or more Yoga teachers to learn the poses, you must develop the teacher within. You are your own best teacher as you cannot get self-knowledge from another. Listening to and reading what others say or have said is beneficial, but real insight, real self-knowledge comes from awareness, awareness of what is going on inside yourself. Rather than following the "experts", use them as resources. In the end, you must follow your heart, but balance it against an educated mind, one that sees and understands various points of view. Yoga is balance. Balance between left and right, front and back, strength and flexibility, internal and external, control and surrender, the critical mind and the compassionate heart.

Find balance each moment through your attention. You find balance by not taking sides; internally or externally. Once you take sides, you are no longer in balance and you cannot see the whole. External conflict is the result of internal conflict. Internal conflict is the result of being out of balance, taking one side against another, being attached to a part without seeing the whole. If you can let go of taking sides, you can relax and experience what is actually happening right now. Balance negates extremes. Extremes require force and force is violence. Peace is balance. It is active and energetic without force.

Past and Present, Pleasure and Pain

By seeking to repeat past pleasures and avoid past pain, we stop living in the present, and therefore cannot experience the new, the real that is unfolding right now. It is easy for many people to discard past pain, but we need to discard past pleasure as well as they go together. Let go of the past. Experience the present. You are only alive right now. This is the quality of mind that is necessary during Yoga practice and it will spill over into your entire life. Do not try to make it happen; just let it happen.

Although we all want to experience pleasure and avoid pain, you cannot have one without the other because pleasure exists only in relation to pain. If you block your perception of sadness and pain, you are also blocking your perception of happiness and pleasure. Develop the heroism to really experience your life, all of it.

Yoga poses remove the tension and blockages from the past that interrupt the balance and flow in the present. Since the mind and body are two parts of the same thing, anything that affects your body also affects your mind and vice versa.

Yoga is not working to perfect more and more difficult poses. Yoga is stretching your body to remove old tensions, reverse compression, and keep your body strong, flexible, balanced, and open. Aging is a normal process, but premature aging is not. It is a result of letting your body and mind get out of balance, closing your mind, body, and heart.

There is an old saying: "Stand on the shoulders of the past". Use the past as a starting point, not an end goal. Knowledge, culture, experience, memory, and thought are all the past. They are not the end, they are only the beginning. They are like the pieces in a board game. Although you need them to play the game, they are not the game. The pieces are static; the game is active and anything can happen. By holding on to the known (the past), you prevent the unknown (the present) in your life. We hold on to the known for security. We are afraid of the unknown and we limit our growth, understanding and joy.

If you are trying to attain a higher spiritual state or trying to "advance" spiritually, you are projecting the known and then trying to "achieve" it; you are trying to capture and hold on to the unknown with the known. (You can only project the past, that which you already know). If you repeat a mental pattern often enough (self hypnosis), you can subjectively experience it, but you are only experiencing your projection and accepting a self-generated illusion for the real thing. The unknown cannot be earned, bartered for, or captured. It comes to you. Just like love and creativity, it only comes when you are open to receive it.

Advanced Poses

Why do you want to do advanced or difficult poses? Is it egotism? Is it competition? Are you willing to injure yourself for a fleeting ego boost? The reason to do a pose is for its benefit. If you are not clear about the benefit of a pose, you may want to omit it until there is a practical reason to include it and work on it. Be honest with yourself. Just as you don't need a complicated tool to hammer a nail into a board, you don't need a complicated pose to stretch your hamstrings. Once your hamstrings are stretched, you don't need an exotic pose to stretch them more. "More" is not balance. Many ballet dancers, gymnasts, and contortionists end up with permanent injuries to their spines and joints. Don't over-do flexibility. Moderation is important in all aspects of Yoga.

Many extreme poses lead to permanent injuries later in life, so just because you are not feeling pain right now does not mean that repetition will not cause damage. As in carpal tunnel syndrome, the damage is a result of repetition. Always be extremely careful with your neck and your knees. They are the two areas that are most often injured as a result of Yoga poses. The point of Yoga practice is awareness and health. If your ego requires more, find it elsewhere, not in your Yoga.

Try not to think of Yoga poses as something that you will attain in the future. It is much more useful to look at Yoga the same way as breathing air, drinking water, and eating food. These are all basic necessities of life. Cats and dogs know this and do Yoga poses throughout the day. You don't try to attain more and more complex or advanced water drinking techniques. As you become more flexible, you will need new poses to stretch your muscles. That doesn't make these new poses better in any way. Once you are at your own healthy flexibility level, you only need to maintain that level. There is really no point in trying to go further as there is no benefit in being hyper-flexible and it can stretch your ligaments, making your joints unstable. The more flexible you are, the less strength you have and vice versa. If you must have a goal, that goal should be balance. Yoga poses are tools for us to learn about ourselves, not trophies to hang on the wall.

Pushers and Pamperers

Many people are either pushers or pamperers in their Yoga practice. While it is healthy to be more aggressive in your practice some days and more restorative other days, it is very important to balance the two. If you pamper yourself too much, you will not improve and if you are too aggressive, you will injure yourself. You need to become aware of your minimum and your maximum edge. Your minimum edge is where you just start to feel the muscles stretching and your maximum edge is the greatest stretch before you feel pain. Be aware of this continuum in each pose. Go slowly from the minimum edge to the maximum. Be good to yourself. "No pain, no gain" does not apply to Yoga. In Yoga it is no pain, no sprain.

Questioning

There are many claims about the great antiquity of Yoga. Many of these claims are quite recent with little or no evidence. The point of this purported antiquity is: What I say has absolute authority because it is based on something, or is the exact thing, that was developed by "god/men" thousands and thousands of years ago. Therefore, who are you to question! The same is true of Yoga teachers and gurus who claim to be part of some unbroken chain of secret knowledge that was passed down from teacher to student for thousands of years. Let the buyer beware!

Yoga is questioning. Questioning authority and questioning yourself. Questioning is healthy as long as it is balanced. Questioning in its extreme can lead to cynicism and a very negative attitude towards others, but a lack of questioning leads to manipulation by all sorts of self-appointed authority figures. Once you accept the authority of another person, book, or system, you stop thinking, stop growing, and give your own responsibilities to another. Self-discovery is the result of taking responsibility for yourself. As J Krishnamurti said, "Truth is a pathless land. There is no path to truth." You cannot get truth from another; you must find it yourself in every moment.

The first step toward learning is to acknowledge one's own ignorance. Learning is a process of questioning not a process of knowing. When you say: "I don't know", you have allowed learning. No matter how much you learn, keep the cup empty, keep your mind fresh and open. Let knowledge and experience flow through you. Do not try to hold on to them. When you hold on to truth and repeat it, it is no longer truth.

Use it or lose it

Our brains are plastic and constantly changing to meet the current need, just like our muscles, bones and other body systems. If you are in weightlessness, you don't need bones to hold yourself up against gravity and therefore your body dissolves your bones and they are absorbed. If you don't use your muscles, they atrophy and are absorbed by your body. Your bones and muscles also get bigger and stronger with increased usage and increased demands being put on them. The more you use your brain and the more varied that usage is, the more neural circuits or pathways you create. A closed repetitive mind reinforces several circuits and lets all the other pathways die away. Our body's cells are constantly dying and new cells are replacing those old ones. If there is increased need, the replacements will be stronger to fit that need. If there is decreased need, the reverse is true. This is why a mindful Yoga practice is so useful. It not only strengthens the muscles, it exercises the mind, breath, bones, nervous system, immune system and all the rest of the human organism.

Yoga is a process

Yoga, just like human consciousness, is a process, not a thing or a place or a belief or a set of practices or a set of rules. Already in the womb, the brain is constantly rearranging itself to deal with its new experiences. Your **mind**/body is constantly re-wiring itself to meet the current need and your **body**/mind is constantly dying and re-building itself to meet its current requirements. Consciousness, the mind and the body are not opposing states or things, they are one undivided process. All states are fluid so trying to hold on to a particular state is like taking one frame out of a movie and trying to play it over and over. Each frame has meaning only in the flow of the entire movie. Life itself is an electrochemical process. As long as we keep breathing in oxygen (the catalyst to this process) and keep breathing out carbon dioxide (the waste material of this reaction or process) we have life.

Homeostasis

Human homeostasis is the process of regulating the internal environment of the body to maintain a stable, constant condition. This is how our body's internal processes maintain balance and therefore health. Many diseases are caused by homeostatic imbalance, including diabetes, dehydration, hypoglycemia, hyperglycemia, gout, anemia, and diseases caused by toxins in the blood. Homeostasis regulates internal body temperature, the amount of iron in red blood cells, blood glucose with insulin and glucagon, the osmotic pressure of bodily fluids, the renin-angiotensin system (which helps regulate blood pressure), calcium in the blood, blood plasma pH, the balance between fluid gain and fluid loss, blood coagulation and sleep cycles. Our external physical and internal mental processes also require balance to achieve and maintain health. Again, Yoga can be an extremely useful practice to help encourage and maintain that balance.

Building Neural Pathways

When we are born, we have a multitude of potential neural pathways in our brains, limited only by our genetics. As we grow and mature, we develop certain paths and use them over and over. The more often a thought, feeling or action is repeated, the stronger the neural pathways become that connect those specific brain cells (neurons). We always do certain things a certain way. We hold our cup the same, eat the same food, think the same thoughts, relive the same old hurts. After a while, these pathways are so ingrained, such deep ruts, that anything new is almost impossible. We are then caught in the equivalent of a computer loop, repeating the same old thing over and over. This is old age. It is optional.

Physical actions are in the present. When you do a new pose, learn a dance or sport, try a new food, or learn to play a musical instrument, you are building new pathways. The new pathways that new actions build will lead to new thoughts and feelings as well. The mind and heart can only grow in a living body. A repetitive, machine-like body stops the growth and without growth, there is premature decay and death.

Mental and emotional responses are also often stuck in the past. How many times do we react to someone or something inappropriately in the present because of an association to some memory? Before you can change a mental/emotional pattern, you must see it clearly. Often people aren't aware of repetitive thoughts and their related emotions and physical reactions. These repetitive thoughts may be impacting their health and happiness and they may be unaware of how insidious they are. This is where the attentive practice of Yoga is important. When your attention is directed to your inner dialogue, these patterns can be clearly seen. Do you blame others? Do you blame yourself? Are you afraid? Do you judge? Do you force? Do you fight? Do you quit? Are you seeking escape? Whatever you do in your Yoga, you probably do in the rest of your life. You are either strengthening these old pathways or building new, more positive pathways. Remember, if you are not growing, you are dying. Let go of the past. The past is dead. You can only grow right now.

Meditation

We experience our perceptions, not what actually *is*. All our perceptions are subjective and we can perceive almost anything that we believe by filtering out everything that does not fit our beliefs. The exterior world projects itself on our minds and our minds project their content on the exterior world. It is vital to perceive our world as objectively as possible and not color our perceptions with our prejudices, both personal and cultural. Only then can we act and react in our own best interest and in the best interest of others and our environment. Direct perception (seeing without editorial comment, judgment, condemnation, identification, memory or desire) is as close to reality as we can get. Once our minds start interpreting, we get further and further from reality.

The observer and the observed are the same. They are both your mind. Even though what you observe may have an independent existence, what you are observing is in your mind, created by your mind. Your thoughts are your mind. The "you" that observes those thoughts is also your mind.

Your eyes see a flower. They don't actually see the flower, but they do see light that is reflected off the flower. Some of that light forms an image which travels through the optic nerve to the brain and is recreated by your mind in your mind. Your mind creates an experience and interprets it, calls it a flower, defines it as a rose, judges its qualities, remembers happy or unhappy memories related to roses, and your body reacts to those memories by tensing or relaxing, secreting various hormones and you experience various emotions. This entire movie that you just created is now stored in your mind and body. It has very little to do with the reality, the flower.

What happens if you see a flower and don't name it, don't use words in your head about it, don't involve memory or desire, just see it? Find out for yourself! This is meditation.

Sitting meditation- Just sit with your eyes closed and see what happens. Do not make anything happen. Do not stop anything from happening. Just watch without comment.

Breath meditation – Sit quietly with your eyes closed and breathe calmly through your nose. Watch and experience the air entering your nostrils, filling your lungs, and exiting. Repeat as long as you want. Just observe.

Listening meditation – Sit quietly, close your eyes, and just listen, really listen to a piece of music or to nature. (Classical music, whether Eastern or Western, usually works best because of its more developed form). Focus on what you are hearing in the present moment.

Science meditation-Sit quietly with your eyes closed and contemplate the vastness of space and the universe, or the worlds within worlds down to atoms and beyond.

Nature meditation-Find a quiet spot in nature. With your eyes open, using the flower technique above, just observe.

Physical meditation-Totally immerse yourself in a creative physical activity with a minimum of mental chatter and maximum openness to discovery. Examples:
Singing or playing a musical instrument
Art
Dance
Intimate activity with a trusted partner

Yoga poses linked into a flow can become meditation in motion.

Your entire life can become a meditation.

I am not giving more specific instructions for meditation as it is important for each individual to find their own. You must experiment to discover. To simply follow another leads to mindless repetition not self-discovery.

Energy

Practicing Yoga poses gives you more energy because it stretches and relaxes tight muscles. When your muscles are tight, it takes a lot of energy to do anything, even to simply stand or sit because you are working against yourself. Although a certain amount of muscle tension is required to do anything, it is more efficient to keep all muscles relaxed that are not needed for that particular action. The problem is residual stress and the muscle tension that it leaves behind. Once this is released, your muscular-skeletal system becomes really efficient, with no wasted effort.

Prana

Yoga literature often refers to prana. Prana is often translated as "life force" and sometimes as "breath" or "energy". It is the same concept as Chi or Qi. Prana includes all types of energy in our bodies and the universe and there are many fanciful ideas about prana that have no known scientific basis. Prana in the air we breathe can be seen as oxygen and prana in the food we eat as nutritional content. Prana in the body includes the electrical energy of the nervous system as well as hydraulic and chemical energy throughout the body. Electro-chemical reactions on a cellular level create energy, an energy that we experience as life.

Gurus

When many people think of Yoga, they also think of gurus. The system of guru (teacher) and followers was developed in ancient times as a way of passing information to others. It was based on the authoritarian political/power structure of king (raja) and subjects as well as master and apprentice in the trades and father and family in the home. Since there were no printed books, no internet, and most people lived in villages, the only way to learn something was to find a teacher. From ancient times until the modern era, the king, the teacher, and the father were absolute authorities. This type of authority frequently leads to abuse and corruption because the authority figure has no feedback and the follower has only one point of view available.

This system is now obsolete, as millions of printed books, the internet, and global travel are available to us. Since the relationship between follower and guru encourages dependency and exploitation, the only reason to follow a guru today is to give your responsibilities to another. We all need teachers, but we need various points of view and to think for ourselves to grow. Otherwise, we are like mistletoe growing on an oak tree. The mistletoe gets all its nourishment from the oak and eventually kills it and they both die.

Today we have the luxury of having vast resources at our disposal. While this seems overwhelming at times, we need to find balance between this wealth of external resources and our internal resources, as this stimulates growth.

Yoga Sutras of Patanjali

The Yoga Sutras of Patanjali are one of six schools of thought of Hindu or Vedic philosophy. Together with the Upanishads, the Bhagavad-Gita and Hatha Yoga Pradipika, the Yoga Sutras are the basis for Hindu yogic philosophy. The book is divided into four chapters containing 195 aphorisms (sutras), which are short phrases designed to be easy to memorize. The Sutras were written somewhere between 200 BCE and 300 CE, although they may have existed earlier in unwritten form. Patanjali is considered to be the compiler, not the author of the Yoga Sutras. Some Yoga practitioners today in both India and the West take a very rigid, fundamentalist view of the Yoga Sutras while others view them as simply an interesting step in the development of Yoga.

The Sanskrit word Yoga, as used by Patanjali refers to a state of mind where thoughts and feelings are controlled. Patanjali is considered the authority on Raja Yoga which seeks to attain enlightenment through control of the mind and the senses. There are problems with this approach because that which is attempting to control the mind is the mind and our senses are a vital part of our feedback system. Repressing thoughts and feelings is generally considered unhealthy today. The word Yoga has also traditionally meant "to yoke" (the root of the Sanskrit word is the same as the English word yoke) or "join" your individual consciousness to the cosmic consciousness. Today, most people translate Yoga as "union", meaning the union of mind, body, and spirit.

The Bhagavad-Gita, thought to have been written between 400 and 100 BCE, lists four branches of Yoga. Karma Yoga: The Yoga of action in the world, Jnana Yoga: The Yoga of wisdom and the intellect, Bhakti Yoga: The Yoga of devotion to God, and Raja Yoga: The Yoga of meditation and control of the mind and senses. Patanjali's eight-limbed concept of Raja Yoga (Ashtanga Yoga) is still the core of practically every Raja Yoga variation that is taught today.

Astanga Yoga – The Eight Limbs of Yoga

I.   Yama (Abstinences)
    a.   ahimsa – non-violence (1.)
    b.   satya – truthfulness (2.)
    c.   asteya – non-stealing (3.)
    d.   bramacharya – celibacy (4.)
    e.   aparigraha – non-possession (5.)
II.   Niyama (Observances)
    a.   saucham – purity (6.)
    b.   santosha – contentment (7.)
    c.   tapas – burning (8.)
    d.   svadhyaya – study of self (9.)
    e.   ishwara pranidhana – surrender to cosmic intelligence (10.)
III.   Asana (Postures) (11.)
IV.   Pranayama (Breathing) (12.)
V.   Pratyahara (Withdrawal of the senses)(13.)
VI.   Dharana (Concentration) (14.)
VII.   Dhyana (Meditation) (15.)
VIII. Samadhi (Super-consciousness) (16.)

Commentary on the Eight Limbs:

1. **Non-violence** - In the Hindu holy book the Bhagavad-Gita, Krishna (the personification of God) tells Arjuna (the hero of this epic) to kill his relatives. Hindu history is just as violent as Christian, Muslim or Jewish history and their holy books are just as bloody. Violence is part of us and is an unavoidable part of life. Birth and death are both often violent. The fight or flight response is a necessary natural response. The problem is not that we respond with violence when our lives depend on it, but rather that we respond with violence when our thoughts, beliefs, or self-images are felt to be threatened, out of greed, or when we are dealing with memories and prejudices, and not actual present physical danger. Although non-violence does not and cannot actually exist (you can't even have the word non-violence without violence), we really could do a much better job of limiting our violence, as we are unnecessarily violent to ourselves, others, and the planet.

2. **Truthfulness** with yourself is paramount because unless you are truthful with yourself, you have no basis for truthfulness with others.

3. **Stealing** is harmful to both the individual and society because it is based on greed and envy and fosters ill will.

4. **Celibacy** – Although many people now translate this to mean non-attachment to sexuality or only having sex with your spouse, the word celibacy, as used by Patanjali, means no sex, period. Some Hindu texts from this period even state that any loss of semen leads to death. The idea behind celibacy is to trade present sexual pleasure for the promise of a higher pleasure later in this life or in some future life. Many faiths or sects try to control sex because it is a very strong basic human instinct. If you can control a person's sexuality, they are much easier to control in other ways, much as a neutered dog is easier to control. Since our sexual instinct is one of our most primal, its suppression usually leads to perversion rather than some kind of holiness or enlightenment. The repression of anything is unhealthy. We need to understand and enjoy our sexuality and use it in a healthy, positive way. After all, it is the way that life is made on this planet.

5. **Non-possession** - This concept is actually non-possession of anything, much like the medieval Christian concept of renunciation of the physical world. Hoarding or acquiring more than you can use is both selfish and wasteful, but the renunciation of the material world is also the renunciation of life. Many now translate this to mean living as simply as possible, although that is probably not the intent. The greedy, neurotic acquisition of more and more is not healthy for anyone, does not lead to balance, and is ruining people's health and the environment. At the same time, the idea of giving up present material goods for imagined future returns is actually even more greedy and neurotic.

6. **Purity** – This concept is based on the idea that someone defines what is "pure" and then you try to *be* that, rejecting how you really are. While cleanliness is great, looking at other people as "unclean," which is part of this concept and the racist caste system, is not. The concept "pure" can only exist in relation to "impure." If you want to be pure, doesn't that unfortunately make everyone with different ideas impure? Isn't the identification with this ideal a basis for racism and violence?

7. **Contentment** is really enjoying what you have and not being resentful about what you don't have. It is necessary for relaxation as well as physical and mental health. We all have the tendency to want more. If we learn to enjoy what we have, our focus shifts from wanting (desire) to enjoying (joy).

8. **Burning** – According to BKS Iyengar in *Light on Yoga,* burning means "the burning of desire to achieve ultimate union with the Divine and to burn up all desires which stand in the way of this goal." This is very rigid and extremist and probably the opposite of non-violence, contentment, and selflessness. You are only strengthening desire trying to achieve this goal, not getting rid of it. It is also the egotistical craving for the ultimate experience and doesn't leave any room for things like compassion, love, and balance.

9. **Study of self** is necessary for real understanding of anything. If you don't understand the observer, you cannot understand what you observe. There is an important difference between introspection with the goal of self improvement and the study of self with the goal of awareness and understanding. If you are seeking self improvement, you are judging and comparing what *is* to what "should be" and not accepting yourself as you are. This leads to self-condemnation,

preoccupation with self, and often depression. If you are seeking awareness and understanding, you are seeing what *is* without comparison to an ideal and are therefore open to insights and deeper understanding. This leads to transformation.

10. **Surrender to cosmic intelligence** - The problem here is: what is this "cosmic intelligence" that we are surrendering to and who defines it? Usually there is a very mortal authority figure that defines and speaks for the "cosmic intelligence." If you have **not** experienced "cosmic intelligence," this is just words. If you **have** experienced "cosmic intelligence," this is just words.

11. **Asana** - Patanjali was referring to sitting postures for meditation not the active postures that are practiced today as there are no written references to active postures until almost one thousand years later. The Sanskrit word asana literally means "seat."

12. **Pranayama** or breathing exercises are generally excellent for mental, emotional, and physical health. Some of the more "advanced" techniques are considered potentially dangerous by some and a qualified teacher is usually recommended.

13. **Withdrawal of the senses** is based on the idea that the senses and pleasure are bad or evil. This concept is based on the belief that the mind and body are not only separate, but in opposition to each other. Mind and body are the same, just as matter and energy are the same. (E=MC2 is not only true "out there"; it is also true "in here".) Isn't the search for enlightenment, bliss, or Samadhi the search for pleasure? Aren't both pleasure and pain important parts of our feedback system? Do not withdraw your senses, develop them, refine them. You are only alive when you are aware. When you see more clearly, when your senses are more acute, you are more alive. This is why we practice Yoga, to develop mental clarity and physical sensitivity.

14. **Concentration** is an excellent practice for sharpening the mind, but concentration also excludes and can become self-violence when you force it. Balance between concentration and the free flow of thoughts is important so that our minds remain open and do not become rigid. When we are involved in creative activity, the mind naturally concentrates without force or coercion.

15. **Meditation** is also an excellent practice and is wonderful for reducing stress and gaining insights. It also needs to be practiced without force and without ambition. Real meditation is not mechanical or repetitive and does not involve concentration or effort. It is simply the expansion of awareness through relaxing, opening your mind and heart, and observing. While exploring your inner world, don't hide from or try to escape from the outer world. Seek balance between the two as they are really one continuum.

16. **Samadhi** - What are you seeking? Special powers? Greater pleasure? Escape? The point of Yoga is balance. Balance in your life right now. Do not be seduced by ideas of higher states, enlightenment, or special knowledge or powers. You can experience altered states from breathing exercises, drugs, lack of sleep, illness or exhaustion. These are generally not higher spiritual states, but your body shutting down due to trauma, too little or too much oxygen, or intoxication (your body reacting to something toxic). Although insight sometimes happens as a result of these "altered states," these same insights happen naturally when we don't try to control our conscious minds so rigidly. The trauma or intoxication is only breaking down the barriers that our conscious minds can no longer maintain because all our energy is needed for more basic life support. Why do you want altered states? What do you want to escape? Do you want to experience God? If God exists, God is our substance, our very being. If you want to experience

That, you need awareness and sensitivity, not special powers or altered states which are escapes from reality, not a path to it. (Again, there is no path to truth). And if on the other hand God does not exist, you are only trying to experience your fictitious mental projections. Stop trying to get somewhere else. Start really living where you are, right now. This moment is the only reality, the rest is not real. This does not mean going out and wildly seeking experience. This means developing increased sensitivity so that you are really alive, right here, right now.

That Patanjali was brilliant for his time is not disputed. That man has discovered much since then is also indisputable. Again, "Stand on the shoulders of the past". There is still much more to discover. Much of the "knowledge" that we have accumulated over the years has subsequently been proven untrue and much of what we are sure of today will be proven untrue in the future. Do not look for answers in old books. Look for questions.

Much of what is commonly called "Yoga philosophy" is Hindu religious philosophy, some ancient and some very recent. You do not need to accept any philosophy or even know anything about it to get the benefits of Yoga. The number system that we use today, as well as the concept of zero and the decimal system come from ancient India and are steeped in Hindu religious philosophy. (Zero being the concept of nothingness or the Buddhist void) Ancient India, like medieval Europe, did not separate religion and science. This doesn't diminish the value or usefulness of these mathematical systems any more than it makes Yoga practices less useful. Some Yoga beliefs or practices may be nothing more than superstition; that doesn't diminish the value or usefulness of the poses, breathing techniques, and meditation. Yoga poses, breathing, and meditation are valid tools for everyone, regardless of their beliefs, religion, or lack thereof. An open, aware, healthy, balanced person is a better Hindu, Christian, Muslim, Jew, Buddhist, agnostic, or atheist.

Hatha Yoga Pradipika

Compiled between the 12th and the 15th century by Yogi Swatmarama, the Hatha Yoga Pradipika introduces specific physical asanas (poses), pranayama (breathing exercises), and other subjects, including chakras, kundalini, and tantric Yoga. Hatha Yoga is what most people in the West associate with the word "Yoga." The Sanskrit word Hatha (pronounced Ha-Tuh) is often translated as Ha = sun and Tha = moon. This implies balance between opposites and wholeness.

Chakras

The word chakra comes from Sanskrit "wheel" or "circle." Some traditional sources describe between five and eight chakras, although most systems today list seven. Chakras are described as wheels of energy aligned in an ascending column from the base of the spine to the top of the head. Prana is said to flow through nadis or meridians from the chakras.

The idea of chakras has caught on with the New Age movement in the West which has added the colors of the light spectrum and a relationship with endocrine system functions.

There is a related concept called kundalini, where primal energy is thought to be lying coiled like a snake at the base of the spine. In tantric (magical) or kundalini forms of Yoga, the goal is to awaken this energy, cause it to rise up through the various chakras until "union with God" is achieved in the Sahasrara chakra at the crown of the head. The theory of seven chakras that most Westerners adhere to comes from the book entitled "The Serpent Power" written by Sir John Woodroffe (1865-1936), alias Arthur Avalon.

Other models of chakras are found in traditional Chinese medicine, Tibetan Buddhism, Jewish kabbalah, and Islamic Sufism.

The seven chakras are:

Sahasrara or crown chakra – The chakra of silence and consciousness. It is thought to be located above the head outside the body.

Ajna or third eye – The chakra of wisdom, time, awareness, and light. It is thought to be located between the eyebrows.

Vishuddha or throat chakra – The chakra of freedom, communication, and growth. It is thought to be located in the throat.

Anahata or heart chakra – The chakra of love, compassion, and well-being. It is thought to be located in the center of the chest.

Manipura or solar plexus chakra – The chakra of power, energy, assimilation, and digestion. It is thought to be located in the center of the abdomen.

Swadhisthana or sacral chakra – The chakra of sensation, sexuality, and creativity. It is thought to be located in the groin.

Muladhara or root chakra – The chakra of instinct, security, and survival. It is thought to be located between the genitals and the anus.

There is no physically verifiable anatomical basis for the existence of chakras, nadis or kundalini. They are much like angels; some people believe that they exist on a physical level; some believe that they are a metaphor for a spiritual reality; some believe that they are simply superstition. Belief in chakras, kundalini, and other occult beliefs are extra baggage. If you want to be free, travel light. You don't need these things and the more baggage you have, the more difficult it is to live in the present moment, to be aware and alive right now.

If you want to be more in touch with God, the cosmos, truth, creative energy, reality, or whatever you call It, you need mental clarity, not a mind weighed down with all sorts of unnecessary concepts. The more concepts you have, the more closed you are to discovery. Don't limit yourself by only experiencing your memory, the past, which is dead, instead of the present, which is alive.

Hatha Yoga Today

The celebrated Indian teacher Sri Krishnamacharya (1888-1989) is the source of many of the modern schools of Hatha Yoga. His most well-known students in the West include Sri Pattabhi Jois, founder of the vigorous Ashtanga Vinyasa Yoga style, B.K.S Iyengar who stresses alignment and the use of props, Indra Devi, and Krishnamacharya's son T.K.V. Desikachar who developed the Viniyoga style. These students of Krishnamacharya (not to be confused with Krishnamurti) have all developed very different styles of Yoga as Krishnamacharya always encouraged each practitioner to fit the Yoga to themselves rather than fitting themselves to the Yoga. Swami Sivananda (1887-1963) and his followers are another major influence. Most major types of Hatha Yoga today owe much to these prominent teachers. Hatha Yoga is still evolving, especially in America.

Some of the most popular styles of HathaYoga practiced in the West today are:

Iyengar Yoga, created by B.K.S. Iyengar, is characterized by great attention to detail and precise focus on alignment. Iyengar pioneered the use of "props" such as blocks, straps, chairs, cushions, and sand bags. His book, *Light on Yoga*, is considered a classic. Iyengar Yoga classes are highly verbal and can be somewhat authoritarian and dogmatic. Students work on one pose, are actively corrected, stop, and then start a new pose. Classes are usually segregated by skill level. There is usually no flow from pose to pose and breathing is usually not a major focus. Special emphasis is put on headstands and shoulderstands and they are often held for extended periods of time. Props are used on a regular basis throughout the class. Both Iyengar and Patanjali are usually devoutly revered in Iyengar classes and self discovery is when you "realize" what Iyengar or Patanjali said, not when you find your own unique voice. Because of the great emphasis on alignment in this practice, many of today's leading teachers have studied with Iyengar (including Rodney Yee, Beryl Bender Birch, Judith Lasater, Ganga White, John Friend, Seane Corn, and Erich Schiffmann), before going on to find their "own" Yoga.

Astanga Vinyasa Yoga is the style of Yoga taught by Sri K. Pattabhi Jois. The asana (pose) sequences in Pattabhi Jois vinyasa (string of poses) are based on Krishnamacharya's book *Yoga Makaranda*. It is a vigorous, aerobic, athletic style of Yoga that was originally taught for teenage boys to release their pent up energy. Astanga Yoga also relies heavily on the philosophy of Patanjali's Yoga Sutras, especially the eight limbs. There are six series of poses which the student, depending on their skill level, always do in the same order with emphasis on breathing. The flow from pose to pose (vinyasa) is used to create heat which increases blood circulation and warms the muscles, allowing greater flexibility and reducing the risk of injury. The different sequences begin with Sun-Salutations and standing poses, called the "opening sequence." The student then does the Primary, Intermediate, Advanced A, B, C, or D sequences depending on skill level and ends with inversions called the "finishing sequence." Astanga Yoga is often taught as "supervised self practice." This practice is too strenuous for many people and some of the poses can be dangerous for the knees. Experimentation is limited to the six sequences and deviations from them are discouraged by many Astanga teachers.

Power Yoga is an American adaptation of Astanga Yoga and is a vigorous, fitness-based style of Vinyasa Yoga. Unlike Astanga Yoga, Power Yoga does not follow a set of poses and classes all differ from one another. The emphasis is usually on strength and flexibility and is often more flexible in its approach than Astanga Yoga. The two Yoga teachers often credited with the invention of Power Yoga are Beryl Bender Birch and Bryan Kest. Another name often associated with Power Yoga is Baron Baptiste, who has his own method. Power Yoga classes (although all different) usually appeal to people who are already fit and want an intense Yoga workout. Chanting, meditation, and philosophy are seldom part of a Power Yoga class.

Flow or Vinyasa Flow Yoga is any type of Yoga that flows from pose to pose like Astanga Yoga. It often combines various elements of both Iyengar and Astanga Yoga, as well as other systems, into a flow with great importance usually given to the breath. Flow Yoga can have almost any philosophical basis as it is more about how you practice your Yoga than what you believe. There are an almost infinite number of possible "Flow" sequences and some practitioners also practice "Intuitive Flow," which is flowing from one pose to the next without any plan whatsoever, following your intuition. In Flow Yoga, you can choose a particular sequence of poses (which you design or which you learned from a teacher) to fit what you need at that particular time. It can be vigorous or calming, fast or slow, athletic or restorative. Classes can be highly structured or free depending on the studio and teacher. The White Lotus Flow Series is a good example of this type of Yoga.

Bikram or Hot Yoga is a style of Yoga developed by Bikram Choudhury. He studied Yoga with Bishnu Ghosh and is part of a different "lineage." Bikram Yoga is done in a room heated to 105° F with a high humidity level. The teacher follows a specific dialogue while talking students of all ages and levels through the ninety minute series of 26 Yoga poses and two breathing exercises. Each pose is done twice and there is a short focused relaxation between each pose. The poses, order, duration, and dialogue are always the same. If you go to any Bikram class in the world, you will get exactly the same class. Because of the heat and humidity, it is a very intense workout and not for everyone. There is generally no specific philosophical point of view offered in Bikram classes.

Anusara Yoga was started by John Friend in 1997 and is a Hatha Yoga style that follows a Tantric (magical) philosophy and emphasizes "Universal Principles of Alignment," "heart opening" in poses, and a New Age spiritual view where "the universe is seen as a manifestation of the Divine, which seeks to experience its own bliss through infinite diversity of form". While too New Age for some, it is exactly what others are looking for. It is more emotional than physical in its approach compared with the other schools mentioned above.

Yin Yoga is also called Taoist Yoga. The fundamental tenet of Taoism is that all things have both a Yin and a Yang aspect, which appear to be opposites although each requires the other to exist. For example, if you are looking at the front of an object, there is also a back to it that you cannot experience at the same time. The front is Yang and the back is Yin. Inhaling is Yang and exhaling is Yin. Muscles are Yang and connective tissue and joints are Yin. While most Hatha Yoga is Yang, emphasizing muscular movement, Yin Yoga targets the connective tissue of the hips, pelvis, and lower spine. Yin postures are held for three to five minutes, are really deep stretching and complement rather than replace the more muscular styles of Yoga.

Choosing a Style and Teacher

Before you can choose a yoga teacher, you need to decide which style of Yoga best fits you. Committing to one primary style of Yoga is good for beginners because mixing different styles at this point will lead to confusion. You need to start with a good solid basis. Take your time and be consistent. As you advance, trying other styles will broaden and deepen your practice. If you don't learn various styles at the intermediate level, you risk becoming narrow in your practice and only learning someone else's Yoga without ever finding your own. Each of the teachers that I mentioned above developed a style of Yoga that worked for them and for their unique students at a particular time and place. Iyengar, Jois, and Desikachar all learned Yoga from Krishnamacharya and each went on to develop their own unique Yoga. (Krishnamacharya taught that the Yoga should fit the student, not the student fit the Yoga.) Even though some may proclaim their style of Yoga to be "universal," it is still "their" Yoga. Do not mechanically follow someone else, no matter how "advanced" they may seem to be. "Stand on the shoulders of the past," including your own past. (Your teacher may tell you not to try other styles, but they really do have a conflict of interest here). Don't become a superficial imitation. You have a unique body, mind, and spirit. Find it. Find "your Yoga." Find it new every day.

To find that initial style that suits you, attend as many different classes as you can in your area. You can also check out videos and DVDs from the public library. Define your objectives and ask the studio how they will meet them. Ask about the studio's Yoga philosophy and instruction philosophy. Many studios will offer a free first class and then after class try to get you to make a commitment. Don't agree to anything or make any financial commitments until you have tried them all and are sure. Don't let a studio's sales pitch influence you. Your body will tell you which is best if you listen.

Once you have decided on an initial style, you need to choose a teacher. There may be many different teachers at the studio you choose or several different studios that you like. The limiting factor when choosing a studio is often proximity to either your home or your work. The limiting factor when choosing a teacher is usually time; which teacher teaches a class at a convenient time for your schedule. If the time is not a good one for you, you will not continue over the long run. Remember, you are not marrying this person, you are purchasing a service. If you aren't happy with one teacher's style, try another. Don't be afraid to ask what training, experience, and certification a teacher has. Once you are happy with your teacher, taking other classes with other teachers is not being unfaithful. Learn a technique from as many different perspectives as possible, then learn as many techniques as possible. Be consistent in your practice. Practice at home as well as in the studio.

Yoga Benefits

Physiological

Endocrine function normalizes
Autonomic nervous system function normalizes
Gastrointestinal function normalizes
Lower pulse and respiratory rate
Improved cardiovascular functions
Lower blood pressure
Increased flexibility and range of motion
Increased strength
Increased energy
Weight normalizes
Increased endurance
Improved posture
Improved sleep
Improved immune system
Reaction time improves
Improved coordination
Improved balance
Improved bone density
Lower rate of injury in sports
EMG activity decreases
Physicians prescribe Yoga most often for:
    Asthma
    Lower back problems
    Stress related illnesses

Psychological

Improved mood and sense of well-being
Decreased anxiety
Decreased depression
Decreased hostility
Social adjustment improves
Attention span increases
Learning efficiencies rise
Memory increases
Impulse control increases

Biochemical

Total cholesterol and triglyceride levels go down
Hemoglobin levels rise
Anti-stress and antioxidant factors increase
EEG-alpha waves increase

Diet

Drink lots of fresh water. (Again, use balance and common sense). Only eat when you are hungry. When you are no longer hungry, stop eating! Take your time and really enjoy your food. Notice how the foods that you eat taste, but also be aware of how you feel later as a result of eating those foods. Try to eat foods with as much prana (life-force) as possible. This means eating plenty of fresh fruits, fresh vegetables, whole grains, legumes, and nuts. While some Yogis condemn the eating of dairy products, eggs, fish, and meat, others include them in their diet. If you do eat fish or animal products, know how and where the animals were raised and what they were fed. Keep animal fat, salted or smoked foods, alcohol, caffeine, and sugar to a minimum. Avoid trans fats, high fructose corn syrup, and unnecessary additives. The important thing is to eat food that has been processed as little as possible. The more processed a food is, the less prana it has. The fresher food is, the better it tastes. Do not smoke! (Burning incense is also smoking as you are breathing smoke just like second hand cigarette smoke.) Don't get radical or rigid about diet as balance in diet encourages balance in the rest of your life.

Yoga injuries

I have not included headstand (Sirsasana), shoulderstand (Sarvangasana), or plow (Halasana) in this book, as these poses often cause compression of the cervical spine (neck) and should only be learnt under the direction of a competent teacher, if at all. They should be avoided altogether if you have neck problems, are overweight, have a weak upper body, have blood pressure problems, diabetes, glaucoma, have had cataract surgery or retina problems, or are severely nearsighted. Some Yoga practitioners permanently injure their necks doing inversions, especially when doing them often and holding them for extended periods of time. While these poses have benefits, those same benefits may be obtained from other poses without danger of injury. To invert your body may be healthy. To support your body weight on your neck is definitely risky for many people. Your neck was designed to support your head weight, not your entire body weight. If you feel any neck compression or pain in an inversion or going into the inversion, check with a competent teacher. You may be doing it wrong or that inversion may not be for you. Even though headstand and shoulderstand are traditionally called the "King" and "Queen" of the poses, we also call one of the most icy spots on earth "Greenland." You only get one neck in this life; take good care of it.

There are also poses like full lotus (Padmasana), hero (Virasana) and reclining hero (Supta Virasana) that are potentially dangerous for people's knees. Again, these poses are not necessary, require a competent teacher, and should be approached with caution. Although many people were able to do full lotus as children, most adults do not have the hip flexibility to do it now. If you cannot bring both knees to the floor in **Cobbler** (Fig 83) with a straight back, you should not even attempt full lotus as you will injure your knees. If you really want to do full lotus, work on **Cobbler**. If your hips aren't flexible enough for **Cobbler**, you must force your knees into excessive internal rotation to get into full lotus. The knee joint is not designed to be internally rotated that far and it will lead to injury. Once you can do **Cobbler** and hold both knees to the floor without stress, practice half lotus until it is totally comfortable and then start on full lotus. Many adults will never be able to do full lotus without risk of injury. Although almost all of the thousands of Yoga poses can be beneficial to someone at some time, you only need to practice those poses which have a low risk of injury and are beneficial to your unique body right now.

Compared to most sports, Yoga injuries are really infrequent. Always taking care of yourself and using both internal (awareness) and external (teachers, mirrors) feedback is the best approach.

Self-Image

The central object of many people's lives is the expansion of their sense of self and their self-image. That is why people are so needy for money, power, fame, and domination over others and the environment. Some people use Yoga as part of this process of self-expansion. The desire for attainment of any type limits discovery. We all have desire. To want to be free of desire is itself a desire. The purpose of Yoga is to increase awareness, self-discovery, and balance. Once you are really aware of your desires, you can understand them. Once you really understand your desires, you are no longer a slave to them.

If you repress desire, it comes back in perverted forms. For example: A man (I'm using man in this example, but it could be the other way around) sets up his Yoga mat for class. He notices a very attractive woman next to him. The man can acknowledge his attraction, decide that although this is a natural desire, this is not the appropriate time or place, let the desire go (through understanding and non-attachment not suppression) and move on with the Yoga class, free to focus on the exercises. -OR- He could not acknowledge or suppress his desire, pretend to be working extra hard on the poses for another reason, and injure himself through inattention to internal feedback while pushing too hard to get approval, attention, and to impress. Your desire is there whether you acknowledge it or not. This is why simply pretending to be non-violent or not to have desire is counter-productive. You then stop acknowledging what doesn't fit your self-image and it controls you unconsciously.

What if we stop looking for approval from ourselves and others to support our self-images? We often seek approval to strengthen our sense of self and our competitive desire to view ourselves as better than others. Both approval and disapproval, whether internal or external, are important feed-back and should be used as such, not as ways to amplify our self-images and competitiveness. If used as feed-back, approval and disapproval are valuable tools; if used to expand our self-image, they are an addictive and dangerous drug.

How do you think of yourself? Do you think that you are smart? How do you deal with it when you act stupidly? Do you think that you are caring? How do you deal with it when you act uncaring? What if you didn't think of yourself in any particular way? What if you just let go of your self-image? What if you stopped trying to be a certain way and just observed how you really are? You are much better off dealing with what actually *is* on a moment to moment basis as you can only transform that which actually *is*. Keeping up that self-image takes an awful lot of energy.

If you are aware of what is going on right now in a nice balanced, relaxed way, you will automatically make the right decisions. It is when you are repressing something and then calling it something else which is acceptable to your self-image that you make bad decisions. Being aware of yourself honestly, right now, does not take a lot of energy. Maintaining an ever-expanding self-image is a full-time job. It makes you fearful and tense because you have to defend it and are always afraid that others will find out that it is only an image and not real. Let fear go. Let love, creativity and the unknown happen. Balance your life with Yoga. Now.

In conclusion

I sincerely hope that this book has stimulated your mind, body, and imagination to find your own Yoga and encourages you on your unique journey of discovery.

Complete Sequence

Fig	Basic	Level II	Level III

Mountain sequence

1	Mountain		
2-4	Extended mountain A		
5	Extended mountain B		
6	Extended mountain C		
7	Crescent moon (both sides)		

Sun salutation

2-4	Extended mountain A		
20	Gentle back bend		
21	Forward bend		
22	Forward arch		
23	Lunge (right foot back)		
24	High plank		
27	Low plank		
28	Up dog		
29	Down dog		
23	Lunge (right foot forward)		
21	Forward bend		
30	Chair		
1	Mountain		

Sun salutation with lunge/plank sequence

2-4	Extended mountain A		
20	Gentle back bend		
21	Forward bend		
22	Forward arch		
23	Lunge (right foot back)		
32		A - Elbows to floor	
33		B – Arms up	
34		C – Back bend	

Fig	Basic	Level II	Level III
35		D – Twist	
23		Lunge (right foot back)	
24	High plank		
36-38		E – Side plank	
39			F – Back plank
36-38		E – Side plank (other side)	
24		High plank	
27	Low plank		
28	Up dog		
29	Down dog		
23	Lunge (right foot forward)		
32		A - Elbows to floor (other side)	
33		B – Arms up	
34		C – Back bend	
35		D – Twist	
23		Lunge (right foot forward)	
24		High plank	
27		Low plank	
28		Up dog	
29		Down dog	
		Jump feet forward	
21	Forward bend		
30	Chair		
1	Mountain		

Sun salutation with triangle sequence

Fig	Basic	Level II	Level III
2-4	Extended mountain A		
20	Gentle back bend		
21	Forward bend		
22	Forward arch		
	Jump (or walk) both feet back		
24	High plank		
27	Low plank		
28	Up dog		
29	Down dog		
40-41	Triangle (right foot forward)		
43		Half moon	
44			Revolved half moon
48			Half moon
40-41			Triangle
45			Revolved triangle
40-41		Triangle	
23	Lunge (right foot forward)		
24	High plank		
27	Low plank		
28	Up dog		
29	Down dog		

Fig	Basic	Level II	Level III
40-41	Triangle (left foot forward)		
43		Half moon	
44			Revolved half moon
43			Half moon
40-41			Triangle
45			Revolved triangle
40-41		Triangle	
23	Lunge (left foot forward)		
24	High plank		
27	Low plank		
28	Up dog		
29	Down dog		
	Jump (or walk) both feet forward		
42	Forward bend (holding elbows)		
1	Mountain		

Sun salutation with side warrior sequence

2-4	Extended mountain A		
20	Gentle back bend		
21	Forward bend		
22	Forward arch		
	Jump both feet back		
24	High plank		
27	Low plank		
28	Up dog		
29	Down dog		
23	Lunge (right foot forward)		
46	Side warrior (right foot forward)		
47	Reverse warrior		
46	Side warrior		
48	Extended side angle	50 Hand to floor	51 Bound
46	Side warrior		
23	Lunge (right foot forward)		
24	High plank		
27	Low plank		
28	Up dog		
29	Down dog		
23	Lunge (left foot forward)		
46	Side warrior (left foot forward)		
47	Reverse warrior		
46	Side warrior		
48	Extended side angle	50 Hand to floor	51 Bound
46	Side warrior		
23	Lunge (left foot forward)		
24	High plank		
27	Low plank		

Fig	Basic	Level II	Level III
28	Up dog		
29	Down dog		
	Jump both feet forward		
49	Forward bend (holding big toes)		
1	Mountain		

Sun salutation with forward facing warrior sequence

Fig	Basic	Level II	Level III
2-4	Extended mountain A		
20	Gentle back bend		
21	Forward bend		
22	Forward arch		
	Jump both feet back		
24	High plank		
27	Low plank		
28	Up dog		
29	Down dog		
23	Lunge (right foot forward)		
52	Forward facing warrior (right foot forward)		
54		Balance warrior	
52		Forward facing warrior	
23	Lunge (right foot forward)		
24	High plank		
27	Low plank		
28	Up dog		
29	Down dog		
23	Lunge (left foot forward)		
52	Forward facing warrior (left foot forward)		
54		Balance warrior	
52		Forward facing warrior	
23	Lunge (left foot forward)		
24	High plank		
27	Low plank		
28	Up dog		
29	Down dog		
	Jump both feet forward		
53	Forward bend (standing on hands)		
1	Mountain		

Standing forward bend sequence

Fig	Basic	Level II	Level III
55-56	Intense side stretch A (right foot back)		
57-58	Intense side stretch B		
55-56	Intense side stretch A (left foot back)		
57-58	Intense side stretch B		
60-62	Wide standing forward bend A		
63	Straddle fold twist		
63	Straddle fold twist (other side)		

Fig	Basic	Level II	Level III
64	Wide standing forward bend B		

Balancing sequence

Fig	Basic	Level II	Level III
65-66	Balanced leg extension (both sides)		
67-68	Flamingo (both sides)	-or- Dancer (both sides)	
69	Dancing Shiva (both sides)		
70			Eagle (both sides)
71-73	Tip toe balance		
74		Balancing hip opener (both sides)	
75	Tree (both sides)		
76	Squat		
77			Crane

Back strengthening sequence

Fig	Basic	Level II	Level III
78	Cobra		
79-80	Lying boat and locust		
81	Bow		
82	Child		
83	Cobbler		

Abs sequence

Fig	Basic	Level II	Level III
84-87	Leg lifts		
88		Boat	
89-90			Boat sit-ups
91	Floor eagle (both sides)		

Seated forward bend sequence

Fig	Basic	Level II	Level III
92	Seated forward bend		
93	Separate side arch		
94-95	Separate leg head to knee		
93	Separate side arch (other side)		
94-95	Separate leg head to knee (other side)		
96	Pigeon A		
97	Pigeon B		
96	Pigeon A (other side)		
97	Pigeon B (other side)		

Back bend sequence

Fig	Basic	Level II	Level III
98	Camel		
99	Bridge		
100-101		Bridge (straight legs)	
102			Wheel
103-4	Cat/Cow		

Fig	Basic	Level II	Level III
82	Child (optional)		

Hip opener/twist sequence

105	Lying bent knee stretch	
106	Lying spinal twist	
105	Lying bent knee stretch (other side)	
106	Lying spinal twist (other side)	
107-8	Lying extended leg A & B	
107-8	Lying extended leg A & B (other side)	
109	Rock the baby	
109	Rock the baby (other side)	
110	Sitting twist	
110	Sitting twist (other side)	

Relaxation

111	Corpse		
	Breathing A	-or-	Breathing B
	Relaxation		

Glossary

Abdomen – The abdomen lies between the diaphragm and the pelvis. It contains most of your digestive, urinary, and reproductive organs. The abdominal muscles are essential for posture and support of the spine. Abdominal breathing is when you extend your abdomen out as your diaphragm flexes down on inhaling and reversing on exhaling. Although the air is only filling your lungs, you have the feeling of filling your abdomen as well. This leads to very deep relaxed breathing. The abdominal muscles can also increase the force of exhalation by contracting and pushing the diaphragm up.

Autonomic nervous system (ANS) - The ANS is the part of the nervous system that controls the involuntary activities of our bodies. These include cardiovascular, digestive, and respiratory functions as well as responses like salivation, perspiration, the diameter of the pupils, and hormonal and biochemical functions. Breathing is normally an ANS function, but can also be consciously controlled.

Diaphragm – The diaphragm is the muscle that separates the thoracic (lung and heart) cavity from the abdominal (digestive and urogenital) cavity. It is crucial for breathing. During inhalation, the diaphragm contracts, pulling it down, the ribs pull up and out, and the resulting reduction in air pressure in the lungs draws air into them. When the diaphragm relaxes, air is exhaled by elastic recoil of the lungs, like a rubber band that is no longer being stretched returning to its former size. The intercostal muscles are also part of this process.

Endorphins – Endorphins are biochemical compounds that are produced by the pituitary gland and hypothalamus that produce analgesia and a sense of well-being.

Intercostal muscles – Intercostal muscles are the groups of muscles between your ribs. When they contract, they pull the ribs up and out, increasing the size of the rib cage and allowing more air into your lungs. When they relax, they help exhalation.

Psoas - Psoas are the muscles that connect the legs and body. They are located on either side of the lumbar spine and connect to the inner thighs. These muscles are essential for lower back support, alignment, and control. Their contraction bends the trunk forward over the pelvis and they help move the legs. It is important to stretch them before doing back bends.

Sciatica – Sciatica is a set of symptoms caused by the compression and/or irritation of one of five nerve roots located in the lower back (L4, L5, S1, S2, or S3) that are branches of the sciatic nerve. It is often very painful and can be felt in the lower back, buttock, and/or the leg and foot. It is usually only felt on one side of the body.

Spinal column – The spinal column is divided into five parts. The first seven (C1-C7) vertebrae (starting from the top) are called the **Cervical** vertebrae, the next twelve (T1-T12) are called the **Thoracic** vertebrae, the next five (L1-L5) are called the **Lumbar** vertebrae, the next five (S1-S5) are called the **Sacral** vertebrae, and the bottom four (Co1-Co4) are called the **Coccygeal** vertebrae. The cervical vertebrae (neck) are small, thin and mobile, allowing the neck to move in all directions. The thoracic vertebrae (upper and middle back) are larger and less mobile and support the ribs and chest or thoracic cavity. The lumbar vertebrae (lower back) are the largest and strongest and support the body from the waist up. The sacral vertebrae are fused, very sturdy, and form the base of the spinal column. The Coccyx or coccygeal vertebrae are also fused and are often called the tail-bone.

Sternum – The sternum (breastbone) is a long, flat bone at the center of the chest. It is connected to cartilage that connects it to the ribs. It is part of the rib cage that encloses the heart and lungs.

Sympathetic and Parasympathetic nervous systems – The sympathetic nervous system is the "fight or flight" system and the parasympathetic is the "rest and digest" system. They function in opposition to each other but are complementary rather than antagonistic in nature. The sympathetic can be seen as the accelerator and the parasympathetic as the brake. The sympathetic nervous system diverts blood flow away from the digestive and reproductive organs, increases the flow to the skeletal muscles and lungs, dilates bronchioles of the lung, increases heart rate, and dilates the pupils allowing more light to enter the eye. All of these actions allow the body to better respond to an emergency. The parasympathetic nervous system does the opposite and returns the body to normal or rest. There is a constant interplay between these two systems to adjust everything from heart rate and blood pressure to breathing and sexual function.

Early Reviews

"Jim Gaudette has created a down to earth manual of yoga practice that is inspiring without being preachy, and full of common sense and wisdom about this art form that is too often misunderstood. His emphasis on safety also sets this book apart. I hope "**Yoga – The Art of Balance**" brings yoga home to a legion of new practitioners. Ultimately their health will improve and their lives may find that elusive balance so difficult to achieve." – Chris Conyers, M.D.

"In "**Yoga – The Art of Balance**", Jim Gaudette offers a user-friendly manual for your yoga practice. Few yoga books do such a wonderful job bringing the many aspects of yoga technique and principles to a popular audience. This book has something for everyone. Filled with easy-to-understand descriptions and photographs, this book makes yoga available to young and old, fit and new exercisers. Jim offers interesting insights on yoga principles and how they can be applied to everyone's life." – Julia Hansen South D.C., US elite athlete 1974-1984, Member US Track and Field Team

"I am impressed with this book. As a beginner at Yoga, it was very evident how easy and informative this book was to me. I was able to easily understand positions because they were described so well. But, my favorite thing about the book is that it will resonate with people who practice Yoga at all levels. I really appreciated the fact that as I get better at Yoga, this book is still very helpful and I'm sure it will continue to be helpful the longer I practice Yoga." – Ty Taubenheim, Major League baseball pitcher

Printed in the United States
131917LV00001B/63-160/P

9 781440 101687